BUILDING A HERITAGE

*Studies for Parents Who
Want to Build a Positive Legacy*

Heritage BUILDERS

J. Otis Ledbetter
Kurt Bruner
John Duckworth

David C. Cook Church Ministries, Colorado Springs, CO—Paris, Ontario

Scripture quotations, unless otherwise noted, are from the *Holy Bible, New International Version* (NIV). © 1973, 1978, 1984 by International Bible Society. Used by permission of Zondervan Publishing House.

4050 Lee Vance View
www.cookministries.com
Cover illustration: Phyllis Pollema-Cahill
Interior illustrations: John Duckworth
Product Manager: Cheryl Crews
Edited by Steve Wamberg
Printed in U.S.A.

ISBN:0-7814-5481-6

1 2 3 4 5 6 7 8 9 10

Contents

About Heritage Builders Association

OUR VISION

To build a network of families, churches, and individuals committed to passing a strong family heritage to the next generation and to supporting one another in that effort.

OUR VALUES

Family—We believe that the traditional, intact family provides the most stable and healthy environment for passing a strong heritage to the next generation, but that non-intact homes can also successfully pass a solid heritage.

Faith—We believe that many of the principles for passing a solid heritage are effective regardless of one's religious tradition, but that the Christian faith provides the only lasting foundation upon which to build a strong family heritage.

Values—We believe that there are certain moral absolutes which govern our world and serve as the foundation upon which a strong heritage should be built, and that the current trend toward value neutrality is unraveling the heritage fabric of future generations.

Church—We believe that all families need a support network, and that the local church is the institution of choice for helping families successfully pass a strong heritage to the next generation.

OUR BELIEFS

We embrace the essential tenets of orthodox Christianity as summarized by the National Association of Evangelicals:

1. *We believe the Bible to be the inspired, the only infallible, authoritative Word of God.*

2. *We believe that there is one God, eternally existent in three persons: Father, Son, and Holy Ghost.*

3. *We believe in the deity of our Lord Jesus Christ, in His virgin birth, in His sinless life, in His miracles, in His vicarious and atoning death through His shed blood, in His bodily resurrection, in His ascension to the right hand of the Father, and in His personal return in power and glory.*

4. *We believe that for the salvation of lost and sinful people regeneration by the Holy Spirit is absolutely essential.*

5. *We believe in the present ministry of the Holy Spirit by whose indwelling the Christian is enabled to live a godly life.*

6. *We believe in the resurrection of both the saved and the lost; they that are saved unto the resurrection of life and they that are lost unto the resurrection of damnation.*

7. *We believe in the spiritual unity of believers in our Lord Jesus Christ.*

Heritage Builders Association
c/o ChariotVictor Publishing
4050 Lee Vance View
Colorado Springs, CO 80918
or call: 1-800-528-9489 (7am-4:30pm MST)
www.chariotvictor.com *or* **www.heritagebuilders.com**

Introduction

You've probably passed on a multitude of traits to your children. Perhaps your son has your jaw. Maybe your daughter has your athletic ability. But have you handed down the things that really matter—things like values, a sense of being loved, an understanding of what God is like?

No matter how many genes scientists map, they'll never find one for love. They'll never find a chromosome that creates respect, faith, or honesty. Those traits aren't hereditary—not in the genetic sense.

But they can be passed along, like family heirlooms. You can create the kind of home environment that nurtures godly qualities, cultivates a biblical view of right and wrong, and prepares your children to thrive in a world you may never see.

If you aren't a parent, your heritage can extend to the children you influence as a teacher, an aunt or uncle, or a family friend.

You can build a heritage—an inheritance worth far more than the financial legacies of the world's wealthiest parents.

In this lively and practical course, based on the book *The Heritage* by J. Otis Ledbetter and Kurt Bruner (Victor Books), you and your group members will discover how to build a heritage that honors God.

As leader, you'll find this course easy to prepare and easy to use. Each forty-five to sixty-minute session includes step-by-step instructions printed in regular type. Each session begins with "Getting Ready," which lists everything you need to do before group time. To help pace yourself according to your available time, there are suggested time frames for each step.

All content is Scripture based. At the beginning of each session plan you'll find a list of the passages to be covered.

Things you might say aloud to your group are in **bold type**. Of course, it's always best to restate things in your own words. Suggested answers to questions are in parentheses.

Each of the thirteen sessions features reproducible resource sheets. In most cases you'll use these as handouts for group members. You may wish to combine them into a "student guide" for each participant and distribute those guides at the outset of the course. It would also work to turn some of the resources into overhead transparencies if you'd like.

Thank you for leading this course. *Building a Heritage* can make a crucial, positive difference in the lives of your group members, their children—and the world they'll inherit.

To Adjust the Length of This Course

This curriculum is easily adaptable if a thirteen-session course is not suited to your schedule.

1) The simplest adaptation is to reduce the course length to ten sessions. Run Sessions 1-10 as described in this book. Offer the information and handouts for Sessions 11-13—the "hands-on" planning sessions to build a family heritage—as course take-home material at the end of Session 10.

2) You may choose to combine sessions together, especially if your regular meeting time runs longer than one hour. Many church mid-week sessions offer a 90-minute time frame. If you use this curriculum for such extended sessions, by using the shorter time limits in each lesson step you can run through two lessons per session, and shorten the number of sessions to six.

Back to the Future

1

Session Aim:

To help group members understand what a biblical heritage is, and how building a solid one will enrich the lives of the children they love.

Connections. Whether it's an elderly gentleman listening to the opinionated talk radio host or a stamp collector on the Internet asking about a rare stamp, we try to stay connected with the people in our lives.

When it comes to our own families, connections are even more vital. In fact, when we are born, each of us enters this world with strong connections to preceding generations. You cannot escape the ties of biology and identity that tie you to your parents and their parents, going back for generations.

But our ancestral connection goes beyond physiological characteristics to link up with a spiritual dimension. God made it clear that He allows the consequences of ancestral sin to impact several generations (Deut. 5:9, 10). On the flip side, He also allows the descendants of those who love and obey Him to reap the positive results of Grandpa's and Grandma's good deeds and obedience to God.

Responsible, loving parents tend to instill the same in their offspring, and they in theirs, and so on. The good is passed from generation to generation just like the bad. If we are smart, we'll find a way to make this principle work for us rather than against us.

—*J. Otis Ledbetter and Kurt Bruner*

Getting Ready

Scriptures:
Proverbs 4:1-6; 6:20-22; 14:26.

1. Decide how far you want to go in turning your meeting place into a "world of the future" (see Step 1). If you're into science fiction, or know someone who is, this could be a fun project to pursue during the week before your meeting.
2. Make copies of "Parental Puzzle" (RS-1A). You'll need one copy for every two group members. Cut the bottom section (instructions to partner 2) from the sheet and put the two parts in separate envelopes. You'll need pencils for this step, too—and Bibles for those who don't bring them.
3. Make two copies of the skit "The Reading of the Will" (RS-1B). Choose a man and woman to act it out and, if possible, give them a chance to practice once before the session. Set up two chairs at the front of the room, facing each other, for the skit.

---

❶ The Time Machine

Objective:
To remind group members that children need help to prepare for the future (5-10 minutes).

Before the session, turn your meeting place into a "world of the future." You can do this as simply or as elaborately as you like. The point is to give arriving group members the impression that they're stepping 20 years into the future—the world in which their children will be adults.

Use one or more of the following ideas to "futurize" your meeting place:
• Add 20 years to this year's date and write that on a large wall calendar. Post the calendar in a prominent place.
• Play a video clip from a movie about the future. (Be sure to choose a segment that isn't offensive.)
• As people arrive, greet them as follows: "Today is (the date twenty years from now). How old are your children now? Your grandchildren? Nieces and nephews? The kids who looked up to you in (this year's date)?"

When the whole group has arrived, explain that you're going to be talking about the future—your children's future.

Let's take a survey. What do you think life will be like for our kids in 20 years? After each of the following statements, stand if you agree. Stay seated if you disagree. If you have no opinion, put your hand over your mouth.

1. **In 20 years, people will live on the moon.**
2. **Our kids will live in a world more peaceful than ours.**
3. **In 20 years, it will be harder to get a plumber when you need one.**
4. **Our kids will have to deal with issues we don't face now.**
5. **Most of our kids will drive solar-powered cars.**
6. **In 20 years, the percentage of Christians in our society will be lower than it is now.**
7. **Jesus will return within the next 20 years.**

8. In 20 years, time travel will become a reality.

Acknowledge any trends you see in the group's responses. Do people seem generally optimistic or pessimistic about the world of the next generation?

Some things about the future are hard to predict. But one thing is sure: Our kids will face challenges and decisions that we might not face now.

What do you think is the best way to prepare them for that?

After listening to replies, point out that during the next several weeks you'll be discovering answers to that crucial question.

❷ On Their Own

Objective:
To help participants understand what a heritage is and why it's important to build one (15-20 minutes).

The purpose of this activity is to help your group members feel the frustration of not being able to solve every problem for those around them.

Ask each person to find a partner. Give Partner 1 in each pair a copy of the top section of "Parental Puzzle" (RS-1A) and a pencil. Give Partner 2 in each pair a copy of the bottom section of the sheet, which he or she must not share with Partner 1. Allow a minute or so for those with the top section to try figuring out the puzzle while those with the bottom section watch helplessly.

Then ask: **Partner 1, how are you doing?**

Partner 2, how are you doing?

Let Partner 2 in each pair reveal the contents of his or her instructions.

Partner 2, how did it feel to do this exercise? (Probably frustrating, since Partner 2 couldn't help.)

How is this like watching a child you love face tough times or a hard decision? (Even if you know more than the child, there's only so much you can do to help.)

We may or may not be around when our kids face problems in the future. Even if we are, we'll have to step back and let them make their own choices. How do you feel about that? (Answers may vary from "terrified" to "relieved," though most group members probably harbor some anxiety about their children's futures.)

There's a way to shape the future, a way to "be there" for kids even if we can't be there in person. Let's find out more about it.

Have a volunteer read Proverbs 4:1-6. As needed, explain that this was written by Solomon, son of David.

How had David tried to shape his son's future? (By teaching him about wisdom and the importance of sticking with the principles learned during childhood.)

What did David believe would happen if Solomon gained wisdom? (He would live, be protected, and watched over.)

Based on this passage, how did Solomon turn out to be like his father? (He believed in the value of wisdom; he taught his sons—and readers—as David had done.)

Have someone read Proverbs 6:20-22. Ask: **What do we learn from this passage that we didn't learn from the first one?** (For one thing, we see that Solomon's mother taught him, too.)

Ask a group member to read Proverbs 14:26. As needed, explain that "fear" of the Lord means reverence and obedience. **Let's say you're a person who fears the Lord. How has that been a "secure fortress" for you?**

In what ways would you like that to be a refuge for your children in the years to come?

After listening to replies, say: **Authors J. Otis Ledbetter and Kurt Bruner want to help parents and others shape children's futures. They call the process "building a heritage." Here's how they describe it in their book,** *The Heritage* **(Victor Books):**

"Every family has a heritage, a legacy passed from generation to generation. In truth, though, the heritage is something few parents really understand. Too many times we are not sure what it is or the impact that it has on our own lives—and on the lives of those we love. Let's begin with a definition: A heritage is the spiritual, emotional, and social legacy that is passed from parent to child...good or bad."

I'll extend that definition to include a legacy passed from any significant adult in a child's life to that child. Ledbetter and Bruner call that "extending your heritage." So any adult can pass on a legacy to a child they influence.

Repeat the definition, letting it sink into the group's consciousness. Then ask: **On a scale of one to ten, with ten highest, rate your confidence that you're leaving the children you love with the best possible heritage—one that will be a refuge for them in the years to come. Hold up the appropriate number of fingers to show your answer.**

If time allows, let two or three volunteers explain their answers before you move to Step 3.

❸ Lost Will and Testament

Objective:

To help group members see the difference between "imposing one's values" and building a heritage (15-20 minutes).

Have two volunteers perform the skit, "The Reading of the Will" (RS-1B). After leading a round of applause for your actors, discuss:

Why do you suppose Mr. Tarbuckle's parents left him such a lousy inheritance?

Do you think most parents today are reluctant to "impose their values" on their kids? Why or why not?

What's the difference between imposing your values on kids and building them a heritage that will be a refuge for them in the future?

Listen to opinions. Then say: **I'm going to read a quote from J. Otis Ledbetter in *The Heritage*. See whether you can pick out key words that help define the difference between imposing values and building a heritage.**

"Like most parents, Gail and I stayed up long nights with Becky when her brow was hot with fever. We carefully doted over her when she was toddling, to keep her from a falling injury. In addition, we shared our deep values in almost every conversation; we spent thousands of dollars to educate her in a place that would uphold our values. We guided her in what to read, what and whom to listen to, how to pick her friends; we taught her what family tradition was like and how valuable the love of a family is when the outside world abandons her. We did everything in our power to protect her developing emotions. All this was part of giving her a heritage."

As needed, point out that words like *doted, shared, spent, guided, taught, protect,* and *giving* spell the difference. (It might help if you write the words on a chalkboard as group members recall them.)

Although the passage we just read might sound too ideal to some of you to ever be realized in your family, building a sound heritage for the children we love isn't beyond any of us. Building a heritage is not simply handing a child a list of do's and don'ts. It's about modeling and sharing values in the context of a loving relationship.

Over the next several weeks, we're going to find out how to do that. We're also going to consider the heritages we've received from our parents—some good, some not so good. We'll want to keep some parts of those legacies to pass along; some parts we'll want to replace. That's because we all want the best for the children we love.

❹ Best Case Scenario

Objective:

To help group members begin thinking of personal goals as they consider building a heritage (10 minutes).

Have people turn to the partners they worked with in Step 2. Ask: **What kind of people do you want your kids to be in 20 years? Tell your partner at least three qualities you'd like your children to have. If you aren't a parent, think of a child you know who might need your influence and answer the question with him or her in mind.**

Allow at least three minutes for partners to share their responses with each other.

Now imagine that you can travel to the future. You can't see the children you just talked about—but you can see their family photo albums. What picture would you most like to see in that album—one that reflects the fact that they've received a strong heritage from you? Tell your partner.

Give partners a few minutes to describe the pictures they envision. If time allows, let volunteers share with the whole group.

As we launch the heritage-building process, I hope you'll keep in mind—and add to—those three qualities you'd like to pass along. I hope you'll remember that picture, too—as a reminder of how you can influence the future by building a solid heritage. Now, talk to your partner and share how you'll try to model at least one of those qualities this week to benefit the child or children you have in mind.

Once more, call attention to the "world of the future" trappings you've put in your meeting place. **In a very real sense we'll be time-traveling during the upcoming weeks—into the past to look at the heritages we received, and into the future to shape the men and women our kids turn out to be.**

If time allows, encourage partners to pray for each other as you begin the process of building a heritage.

The Good, the Bad, and the Ugly

2

Session Aim:

To help participants evaluate the heritages they've been given, and to decide which parts to pass along, discard, or change.

It just doesn't seem fair, does it? Some were given a wonderful, healthy, positive heritage—a beautiful gown. Others were handed rags. Many of those who were given a solid heritage will find the process of passing on that tradition as natural as breathing. Others who received a very weak heritage will have no idea how to overcome the past, let alone create a positive future for the next generation.

The good news is that both can create and give a wonderful heritage. Yes, the process of doing so will be much harder for some than others; but it can be done. How? By reclaiming what you lost, or by learning to give what you didn't get.

In this session we will introduce several key principles and practices that can help you to give an inheritance of love. We will help you better understand your own heritage with three self-evaluations. And we will examine the impact of emotional, spiritual, and relational "hand-me-downs."

We all wear them...our goal is to make our heritage work for us rather than against us by discussing several steps for overcoming the bad while embracing the good.

—J. Otis Ledbetter and Kurt Bruner

Getting Ready

Scriptures:

Genesis 37; 45; Deuteronomy 5:9, 10; II Timothy 1:5.

1. Prepare a short length of each of the following for Step 1:
   • rope nearly (but not completely) cut in two,
   • intact rope,
   • kite string, and
   • three lengths of kite string woven together into one cord.
2. Bring a handheld microphone for Step 2, along with Bibles for those who might need them.
3. Copy the three reproducible resources, "Spiritual Legacy Evaluation" (RS-2A), "Emotional Legacy Evaluation" (RS-2B), and "Social Legacy Evaluation" (RS-2C). You'll need a copy of each sheet for each group member. Bring pencils, too.
4. Bring three boxes of clothing for the Step 4 activity. The first should have very nice clothes, the second rags, the third a mixture.
5. Make copies of "The Heritage Mixer" (RS-2D), one for each household represented.

❶ Family Ties

Objective:

To help group members see that we've all received heritages of varying strengths and weaknesses, and that knowing those strengths and weaknesses can be important (5-10 minutes).

Before the session, prepare short lengths of the following:
1) a rope nearly severed in half at its middle, 2) an intact rope, 3) a kite string, and 4) three lengths of kite string woven together into one cord.

To start the session, place the four items listed on a table in front of the group. Ask three group members to come up and eevaluate each length of string or rope without pulling on the ends of the strings or ropes. Direct them to place the items from left to right on the table in order of desencing strength. Have them describe as a group what strengths or weaknesses in each item caused them to decide as they did.

Thank the volunteers for their "ratings," then ask the whole group: **What strengths or weaknesses do you see in the items on the table? Anyone care to test the group's "strength ratings" by pulling on the ends of these?**

Ask for one volunteer to test the strength of each item by pulling on its ends. Encourage the volunteer not to worry about breaking the items. After each items is tested, ask the volunteer to rank them in order of descending strength. Thank the volunteer.

Point out that the heritage we've been given—that is, the spiritual and emotional and social legacies passed on by our parents—are part of our "family ties." **Have you ever thought about the strengths and weaknesses of the heritage you've been given? Why or why not?**

What might happen to someone who doesn't appreciate a heritage that is really strong? (He or she probably wouldn't benefit from it, and probably wouldn't pass it along.)

What might happen to someone who overestimates the strength of a heritage that has substantial weaknesses? (He or she might fail to change patterns that need changing, and might pass along faulty values to the next generation.)

We need to get a sound appraisal of the heritage we've received. That heritage can affect us in ways we don't even realize, both in its strengths and weaknesses.

❷ Tacky Talk Show

Objective:
To help participants understand that even though our families and heritages aren't perfect, God can bring good out of the bad (15-20 minutes).

Have a volunteer read aloud Deuteronomy 5:9, 10. Ask: **How do the sins of the fathers (and mothers) affect their children these days? Can you think of examples in the news or in your experience?** (Children of abusers may abuse their children; children of addicts often develop similar addictions; victims of childhood molestation grow up with inner turmoil; etc.)

Have you ever seen the other principle in this passage at work— the one stating that generations reap the benefits of ancestors who loved and obeyed God?

After hearing replies, have the group turn to II Timothy 1:5. **What's the example here?** (Timothy had been influenced by a godly mother and grandmother.)

Does this mean that only those with a solid heritage will make it, and if you have a less-than-stellar family history, you're condemned to repeat it? Let's find out.

Explain that everyone in the group is about to be a guest on a daytime TV talk show. To prepare, everyone needs to read Genesis 37. Assign individuals to play the roles of Jacob (Israel), his wives Bilhah and Zilpah, and Joseph. The rest of the group should represent Joseph's brothers.

After giving people time to read the chapter, pick up a handheld microphone and start playing the part of the talk show host:

Ladies and gentlemen, welcome to Tacky Talk. Today's topic: "Favorite Sons and the Brothers Who Sell Them into Slavery."

Bring your microphone over to the group member playing Jacob and ask: **Would you say you have a dysfunctional family? Why or why not?**

Ask Bilhah and Zilpah: **Do the authorities know you're both married to the same man? Who's your favorite son?**

Ask a couple of brothers: **What do you think of Joseph? Is it true you tried to kill him?**

Ask Joseph: **Aren't you responsible for all this? Do you have some kind of superiority complex? And what's the deal with the flashy coat?**

Ask a brother: **What happened out there at the cistern?**

Ask Jacob: **How did you feel when they told you Joseph was dead?**

Ask the whole "family": **Why are you people so messed up, anyway?**

After fielding replies, end the "talk show": **Counselors are standing by to help the entire Jacobson family, though I doubt they can. Next week's topic: "Disobedient Prophets and the Great Fish Who Swallow Them." Drive safely!**

Thank everyone for participating. Then ask: **What do you think would eventually happen to a family like this? Why?**

Check out what did happen. Have the group turn to Genesis 45 and scan it as quickly as possible. **Did the family fall apart? Did everyone end up starving or murdered or in prison?** (No; Joseph rose to a position of power in Egypt and used that power to help his family.)

What changed the usual pattern here? (God had a plan for Joseph, and Joseph cooperated with Him; God brought good out of a bad family background.)

❸ Family Tree Trunks

Objective:
To help group members evaluate the heritage they've received (15-20 minutes).

Even Bible heroes like Joseph had to deal with their heritage. How about you? How would you describe the heritage you received? Let's spend some time evaluating that heritage.

Give each person a pencil and a copy of "Spiritual Legacy Evaluation" (RS-2A), "Emotional Legacy Evaluation" (RS-2B), and "Social Legacy Evaluation" (RS-2C). Let group members work on these individually.

When people have tallied their scores for each sheet, read this note from J. Otis Ledbetter and Kurt Bruner, authors of *The Heritage*:

"If your score ended up near the bottom, don't despair. There are many who have established and passed a wonderful heritage despite falling into this category. Most of us will probably fall somewhere in the middle…. More likely than not, we received a mixed bag.

"Whatever your specific score, the goal is the same. We hope to better understand our own heritage so that we can keep and pass on the good, and replace the bad with something better."

If volunteers want to share results of their evaluations, let them do so as time allows. Avoid pressing anyone to reveal what he or she may see as an embarrassing family secret, however.

Note that in future sessions you'll talk more about how to overcome a weak heritage. For now you may want to pass on these principles from *The Heritage*:

1. *Watch out for jealousy.* The fact that it's easier for others is beside the point. Give the extra effort to make it work for you, too.
2. *Watch out for anger.* Jesus Christ is in the business of fixing that which is

broken. He offers us the opportunity to start anew. As long as we fixate our attention on the broken parts of our heritage, we will never move forward.

3. *Pray.* Giving what you didn't get requires wisdom, strength, and release of feelings like anger and despair. All of these come through prayer.
4. *Plan.* A good heritage doesn't just happen. This is especially true of those who have no solid model to follow, who seek to break a negative cycle.
5. *Persevere.* The key to finishing the race is not talent, but tenacity. It does not require experience, but endurance.

❹ Dress for Success

Objective:
To help participants begin choosing which parts of their heritage "wardrobes" to wear, and which parts to replace (10 minutes).

Form three teams. Announce that you're going to have a Best-dressed Contest. Each team must choose a representative to dress in one minute, using clothes you've brought.

After the representatives are chosen, give each team one of three boses you've prepared: the first with very nice clothes, the second with rags, the third with a mixture. At your signal, teams start dressing their representatives (over the clothes they're already wearing, of course).

When the minute is up, call a halt to the dressing. Choose a winner and lead a round of applause for him or her.

Then discuss: **What were the biggest challenges in this contest?** (There may have been several, but one was finding good-looking clothes in a batch of rags.)

This contest was a little like the challenge we face in building a heritage. As the authors of *The Heritage* point out, we all wear hand-me-downs. Some of us have received legacies that are like royal robes or gowns; others have been handed only rags. Many of us have both in our wardrobes. But we all have the freedom to choose what we'll wear and what we'll pass on to the children we love. We can decide what to keep and what to replace.

Call group members' attention to the evaluations they completed in Step 3. **In the time that remains, take a look at your evaluations. When you see an area of strength, draw a box around it. When you see a weakness, circle it. This may help you decide which parts of your heritage are worth wearing, and which need to be altered or tossed. This week, consider one thing you can do to help strengthen a positive aspect of your heritage.**

As you wrap up the session, make copies of "The Heritage Mixer" (RS-2D) available to those who would like to work on blending their heritages—overcoming differences in the way spouses were raised. Encourage spouses to work on this sheet during the week for their own benefit. Close in prayer, asking God to help group members value accurately the legacies they've been handed, and to help them choose their "wardrobes" wisely.

Mission: Impossible?

3

Session Aim:

To let participants acknowledge their misgivings about heritage building, and to assure them that they will not be alone in the process.

Neither Paul nor Joann was handed a decent heritage, but they desperately want to begin one for their kids. They have questions…

"Is it possible?"

"Is it too late for us?"

"Are we wasting our time to even try?"

"How difficult will it be?"

"Does this heritage thing really work?"

They will learn that it is possible, it's rarely too late, and "this heritage thing" has lasting rewards that—bottom-line—do work.

The last thing we want to do in this course is give the mistaken impression that building, handling, and passing a heritage is a walk in the park. The principles may be simple, but the task is by no means easy. It requires lots of time and energy. It allows little rest. There will be frequent periods when you will be tired—bone tired!

But it is rewarding.

—J. Otis Ledbetter and Kurt Bruner

Getting Ready

Scriptures:

Deuteronomy 11:18-21; Psalm 78:2-7; Romans 8:26-28; I Corinthians 15:58; Philippians 1:4-6; 4:13, 19; I Thessalonians 5:24.

1. Make two copies of the skit, "Just One More Thing" (RS-3A). Choose a man and woman to act it out and, if possible, give them a chance to practice once before the session. Set up two chairs at the front of the room, facing the group, for the skit.
2. Bring a loaf of bread, a jar of peanut butter, four butter knives, five paper plates, and a roll of paper towels for the Step 3 activity. You'll need a table, too.
3. Make copies of "Objection, Your Honor!" (RS-3B). You'll need a copy for each group member. Bring Bibles for those who don't have them.
4. Bring lemons—one for every 10 group members—for Step 4. If you can't find fresh lemons, lemon-shaped lemon juice containers would be fine.

❶ No Can Do

Objective:

To let group members admit that their busy schedules and past failures may make them less than enthused about trying to build a heritage (10 minutes).

Have two volunteers perform the skit, "Just One More Thing" (RS-3A). After leading a round of applause for your actors, discuss:

Have you ever felt this way, even a little? When?

If you did all the things a Christian is "supposed" to do, based on the advice of self-help books, radio and TV shows, church leaders, and groups like this one, how many hours a day do you think it would take?

For the next couple of minutes, get together with one or two other people. Each of you should complete the following sentence for the others in your group: "So far, my honest reaction to this heritage-building idea is..."

After small groups have discussed this, let volunteers share results with the whole group. Encourage openness, even skepticism, about the practicality of heritage building.

If building a heritage is just one more impossible demand on top of all the others, another kind of spiritual "busy work," it's not worth pursuing. But if it's vital to the well-being of the children we love, maybe there's a way to make it work.

That's what this session is all about.

❷ I Didn't Sign Up for That!

Objective:

To help participants understand what God has and has not called us to do in building a heritage, and that He doesn't leave us alone in the process (15-20 minutes).

Have volunteers look up the following passages: Deuteronomy 11:18-21; Psalm 78:2-7; Romans 8:26-28; I Corinthians 15:58; Philippians 1:4-6; Philippians 4:13, 19; I Thessalonians 5:24. Each passage should be read aloud one at a time and discussed; use the following questions and comments as a guide.

Deuteronomy 11:18-21

How were God's people to teach their children His commands? (They were to talk about them during the normal course of the day, while doing things like sitting at home and walking along the road. There are also instructions here to use reminders like tying commands to hands and writing them on doorframes, which appear to be for the benefit of the adults as much as the children.)

Based on this passage, would you say that building a heritage is possible in everyday life, or is it just for people who have a lot of time to spare? Answers may vary. Point out that even though planning is critical in heritage building, many of those plans can be carried out as part of the activities families do anyway—traveling, sitting down to eat, getting tucked in at bedtime, having a "game night," etc.

Psalm 78:2-7

How was the psalmist planning to build a heritage? (By telling stories of what God had done, and by teaching God's commands to his children.)

What was the alternative? (Hiding these things from his children.)

Did the psalmist seem to see heritage building as a difficult chore? Why or why not? As needed, note that the writer seemed to view much of the heritage-building process as a matter of opening his mouth and telling the truth instead of keeping it inside. He also seemed highly motivated, convinced of the need to pass along a heritage so that the truth wouldn't be forgotten—and so that his descendants would have a good relationship with God.

Romans 8:26-28

Let's say you're overwhelmed by this whole heritage idea. You barely understand what it is, let alone seeing how you can make it work. What help does God offer you here? (His Holy Spirit makes up for our weakness, even compensating for our confusion over what to pray for; He promises to ultimately bring good out of our efforts to obey His instructions.)

I Corinthians 15:58

Your child is two years old. You've got at least 19 years of heritage

building left, and the thought is depressing. **How could this verse help?** (The work may be hard, and we may be tempted to quit. But if we stick with it, it won't be pointless—because we're doing it for the Lord.)

Philippians 1:4-6
Life is so uncertain; you might die before your kids are grown, and they might wander away from the faith. Why start something you may not be able to finish? How could this passage apply? (God is the One who begins a relationship with a child, and He is the One who brings that relationship to its completion. He will always be there, even if we aren't.)

Philippians 4:13, 19
You feel you don't have the time, the energy, the support system to take on this heritage stuff. What help does God offer? (His strength and unlimited resources.)

I Thessalonians 5:24
You're tired of being assigned task after task and being told you have to do them all in order to be a good Christian parent. What might this verse say to you? (If God has called you to build a heritage, He will enable you to answer that call. You may need to separate what God has called you to do, however, from the advice and demands you hear from others.)

❸ Spread Too Thin?

Objective:
To help group members overcome their doubts about building a heritage (15-20 minutes).

Ask for four volunteers. Bring them to a table at the front of the room, where you've placed the ingredients and equipment for making peanut butter sandwiches. Make a sandwich of your own and put it on a paper plate.

Tell the first volunteer: **Your job is to make a sandwich that looks exactly like the one I made.**

Tell the second: **Your job is to make a sandwich without using a knife.**

Tell the third: **Your job is to make a sandwich in 10 seconds.**

Tell the fourth: **Your job is to make a sandwich that's absolutely perfect.**

Put the peanut butter jar in the middle of the table and let your volunteers go to work. When the crumbs stop flying (or in two minutes, whichever comes first), call a halt. Have the volunteers display their creations for the group.

Ask the four sandwich makers about the problems they encountered and how they feel about the results. Chances are that the first person was unable to match your sandwich exactly; the second person found the lack of resources (a knife) frustrating and messy; the third person was rushed and unsatisfied with the results; the fourth was unable to reach perfection.

Thank your volunteers and say: **Some of us may try to approach building a heritage in the same way these folks had to approach building a sandwich. Anybody know what I mean?** (Some think they have to do it the same way someone else does; some try to do it without resources or help; some try to rush it; some think they have to do it perfectly.)

No wonder some of us have doubts about whether we can build a heritage. The fact is that we don't have to copy someone else's way of doing it; we don't have to do it without the proper tools; we don't have to do it in 10 seconds; and we don't have to do it perfectly.

Pass out copies of "Objection, Your Honor!" (RS-3B). Give group members time to look it over. Then ask: **Which objection on this sheet hits closest to home for you?**

Based on the Bible passages we studied, and on your own experience, what advice would you add to that on the sheet?

If participants have advice to add, encourage group members to write it on the backs of the handouts.

❹ Lemon Pledge

Objective:

To encourage participants to be realistic in their heritage-building expectations, help one another in the process, and rely on the resources God provides (5-10 minutes).

Have you ever heard the saying, "If life gives you lemons, make lemonade"? What does it mean? (Make the best of whatever situation life hands you.)

You may feel that when it comes to building a heritage, you have nothing but lemons. You don't have enough time, enough energy, enough experience. God knows about your situation and is ready to help. He doesn't call us to do something without giving us the means to do it.

In the case of this group, what resources might be available to help us with heritage building?

As needed, supplement replies with suggestions like these:

- Each of us has access to God's power through prayer.
- Some group members may have tips to share, based on their childrearing experiences.
- We can support each other, sharing frustrations and victories.
- Books like *The Heritage* contain ideas that keep us from having to start from scratch.
- Others in the church may be willing to help—a man serving as a role model for a single mom's son, for example.
- You'll share ideas from the "heritage tool chest" with the group in future sessions.

Right now, think of the one resource you'd most like to use to this week to help you build your heritage. Don't forget to use it!

Bring out one or more lemons you've brought—one for each 10 or so group members. **We're going to close this session by taking the "Lemon Pledge." I'm going to pass around these lemons. When one comes to you, please pledge silently that you'll do three things when it comes to heritage building:**

- **You'll be realistic in your expectations, not trying to do it perfectly or just like someone else.**
- **You'll help the rest of us through the process.**
- **You'll rely on the resources God provides.**

Pass around the lemons. Then close in prayer, thanking God that the heritage-building mission he's called us to isn't an impossible one.

UNIT 2: DESIGNING MY HERITAGE

Soul Providers

4

Session Aim:

To help each group member evaluate the spiritual heritage he or she is building, and compare it to the one he or she would like to build.

We've all heard the comments:

"I'll let my children decide for themselves when they grow older."

"I don't want to be a hypocrite."

"I hated all that church stuff growing up, so I'm not going to force it on my kids."

Such comments highlight a fundamental misunderstanding of spiritual realities in our culture. We have compartmentalized our spirituality and extracted it from the rest of life. That is tragic and dangerous. Unseen realities influence our daily decisions. When we fail to clarify and reinforce them for our children, we rob them of a critical element in decision making and a vital part of their heritage.

Every heritage includes spiritual, emotional, and social components. Let's begin by inspecting the spiritual. We are, first and foremost, spiritual beings. No heritage is complete, or healthy, unless it has been built upon a spiritual foundation.

—J. Otis Ledbetter and Kurt Bruner

Getting Ready

Scriptures:

I Samuel 3:1-10, 19;
Psalm 8:2; Mark 10:13-16.

1. Bring a magazine photo of a celebrity; put it in an envelope so group members don't see it before they're supposed to. You'll also need enough sheets of paper for the whole group, a supply of pencils, and Bibles.
2. Make three copies of the skit, "Wake-up Call" (RS-4A). Choose a man and woman to play the parts of Eli and Samantha, and someone to act as the Voice. If possible, give your actors a chance to practice once before the session. Set up two "beds" at the front of the room—two tables or two rows of three chairs each.
3. Copy the reproducible resource you used in Session 2, "Spiritual Legacy Evaluation" (RS-2A)—one copy per group member. You'll be using this sheet in a different way this time.
4. Copy the reproducible resource, "What It Is" (RS-4B)—one copy for each group member.

❶ Hard Copy

Objective:

To help participants see that giving children an accurate view of God and spiritual concerns doesn't happen automatically (5-10 minutes).

Start the session with a visual version of the old "Gossip" game. Give each person pencil and paper. Take out a magazine photo of a celebrity and show it only to the first person seated in each row. That person has 15 seconds to sketch the celebrity and show the drawing to the next person in the row. That person does a sketch from the first person's drawing, and so on down the line. No one is allowed to speak.

When everyone has drawn a picture, hold up the last sketch done in each row. See whether anyone can guess who the celebrity is (those who saw the photo must not guess). Then hold up the photo. Give participants a couple of minutes to pass the drawings around, observing how the image of the celebrity "degraded" as it was passed along.

Ask: **Why don't all the sketches look like the person in the photo?** (People's drawing ability differs; most drawings were based on other drawings, which weren't necessarily accurate.)

How is this like the process we go through when we try to give our kids a view of what God is like? (Our image of God may not be accurate, especially if it's copied from other people's inaccurate images.)

How do you know you're giving the children you love an accurate view of God and spiritual things?

This may be tough for group members to answer. If so, simply note that you'll be considering that question in this session.

❶ Do You Hear What I Hear?

Objective:

To remind group members that children are spiritual beings, and that adults need to create an environment in which children can connect with God (15-20 minutes).

Have a volunteer read I Samuel 3:1-10, 19. Then ask: **Does it strike you as strange that God spoke to a child here? Why or why not?**

If this story were taking place today, it might go something like this. Have the actors you've chosen perform the skit, "Wake-up Call" (RS-4A).

After applauding their performances, ask the group: **What was the father's attitude toward the spiritual world?** (That it wasn't as real as the physical world.) **Toward his daughter's connection to it?** (He doubted her ability to make any judgments about spiritual things.)

Do you think this attitude is typical among adults? Why or why not?

Let's see how valid this attitude is.

Have a volunteer read Psalm 8:2. Ask: **Have you ever heard a child praise God, perhaps in a song or a prayer of thanks? What could adults learn from the way children praise God?**

Have someone read Mark 10:13-16. **How does a little child tend to "receive the kingdom of God"?** (With an open mind, humbly, etc.)

What responsibilities does Jesus assign to adults in this passage? (To let children come to Him, to not stand in their way-and to receive the kingdom of God as a child would.)

J. Otis Ledbetter and Kurt Bruner, authors of *The Heritage*, have this to say:

"Eli understood the unseen reality of the spiritual world and knew how to help Samuel connect with God's voice. Parents have the same responsibility when it comes to their children. We must first be sensitive to God's voice ourselves...know how to recognize it...and then create an environment which allows our children to do the same. The end result? They will know the Lord."

Invite group members to react to this quote. Some may question whether children raised in the right environment will always "know the Lord." Explain that the authors are talking about "knowing" God in the sense of recognizing His voice. They are not guaranteeing that children will never reject a sound spiritual legacy. Our job is to create an environment in which children *can* know God—and trust Him for the results.

Ask: **Are we creating that kind of environment in our families? Let's find out.**

❸ Secondhand Survey

Objective:
To help participants evaluate the spiritual legacy they're building (15-20 minutes).

Give each person a copy of "Spiritual Legacy Evaluation" (RS-2A). You probably used this handout in Session 2, when group members evaluated the legacies they've received. This time you want them to complete the form as their children might 20 years from now, based on the way group members have dealt with spiritual issues at home so far. (Note: Group members with no children at home should complete the form on behalf of children in their extended families.)

After people have completed and scored the evaluations, see whether anyone wants to comment or share results.

Then say: **If your score isn't quite where you'd like it to be, you're not alone. Many adults are confused about what a spiritual legacy is, much less how to build one. Here's what the authors of** *The Heritage* **have to say.**

Pass out copies of "What It Is" (RS-4B). Read the first section aloud. Then ask: **Would you like it better if this said, "A spiritual legacy consists of helping your child to receive Jesus as Savior and forming habits of consistent church attendance, Bible reading, and Christian service"? Why or why not?**

Read the second section aloud. Ask: **Based on the way you filled out the evaluation form just now, which of these elements of a strong spiritual legacy do you most need to work on with the children you love?**

Read the third section aloud. **How do adults tend to separate the spiritual from the "practical"?** (By relegating spiritual concerns to church activity times; by urging kids to choose financially lucrative careers over unselfish ones; by using a solemn or even singsong voice when they talk to kids about spiritual things, etc.)

If it's true that our kids will receive most of their spiritual legacy by observing us in everyday life, how does that make you feel? Answers will vary, but many participants may wish they could get their spiritual "acts" together before children start watching.

❹ My So-called Spiritual Life

Objective:
To help each person evaluate his or her own relationship with God before trying to pass it on (10 minutes).

Have group members close their eyes. Explain that you're going to ask some personal questions; there's no need for people to answer aloud. Pause after each question, giving participants time to think.

Think of the mental picture you have of God. Maybe you think of Him as a grumpy old man, a distant king, a buddy, a flash of light, or something else.

If you could duplicate the image you have of God and make it the image your children have of Him, would you? Why or why not?

Now think about your current relationship with God. When was

the last time you talked with Him? Are you tending to run toward Him or away from Him these days? Is the relationship warm? Chilly? Is it active, or just a memory?

If you could transplant your current relationship with God directly into the soul of a child you love, would you? Why or why not?

Have group members open their eyes. If anyone would like to share thoughts he or she had during the exercise, that's fine—but don't press anyone to do so.

In future sessions we'll discuss the "how" of passing along our spiritual legacy. For now, let's concentrate on what we have to pass along. Perhaps you found during that meditative exercise that your image of God and relationship with Him need some repair before you'll feel comfortable about being an object lesson for your (or other) children.

Ask people to close their eyes again.

Think for a moment. What view of God would you like the children you love to have?

If that's not the view of God that you have, what stands in the way? Anger? Guilt? Something else?

What kind of relationship with God would you like the children you love to have?

If that's not the kind of relationship you have with Him, what stands in the way? Something you've done? Something you feel He didn't do?

For the next minute or so, please talk to God about your image of Him and your relationship with Him. You don't have to be perfect to be a spiritual model for kids—but you'll be a happier one if you're honest with God first.

I encourage you to take ten minutes or so this week to talk with a friend about images and relationships that impact your heritage. Give group members time to pray silently before closing in prayer yourself. If possible, alert participants to counseling resources your church offers if they'd like to talk with someone about repairing their images of and relationships with God.

Nothing Less Than Feelings

5

Session Aim:

To help group members understand what constitutes a healthy emotional legacy, and to motivate them to leave such a legacy for the children they love.

The radio tower at Detroit's Metropolitan Airport cleared Flight 255 for departure. The plane hurtled down the runway but did not rise at the normal point. Instead, it continued hundreds of feet further before lifting almost fifty feet. In the cockpit, a computer-generated voice repeated the words, "Stall…stall," indicating that the airflow over the wings was no longer sufficient to lift the plane; the jet was falling, not flying. The plane plunged to the ground.

Though more than one hundred died in the crash, a small child survived when her mother responded by intentionally wrapping the child's tiny body in the protective blanket of her own. Recognizing that she couldn't stop the tragedy from occurring, she did her best to engulf her daughter in an environment that would increase her chances for survival.

A strong emotional legacy can do much the same. It creates an environment of love and protection, increasing the odds for our children as they face the inevitable traumas of life.

Tragedy will come. Painful experiences will invade our desire to protect them. Like that little girl's mother, we can do nothing to stop the collision. But we can help our kids survive, and even thrive through it all.

—*J. Otis Ledbetter and Kurt Bruner*

Getting Ready

Scriptures:

I Corinthians 13:4-8;
Colossians 3:12-14.

1. Bring one tray of frozen snacks and one tray of similar snacks that you've heated (see Step 1).
2. Copy the reproducible resources "Home Inspection" (RS-5A) and "Just in Case" (RS-5B)—one copy for every two or three group members.
3. If you have time and want to add a visual aid to Step 3, bring any kind of nonfunctional but exotic-looking contraption you can cobble together from spare parts.
4. Bring pencils and Bibles.

❶ Mr. and Mrs. Freeze

Objective:

To help group members understand what a strong emotional legacy is and the difference it can make in a child's life (10-15 minutes).

Before the session, buy enough frozen snacks—the kind intended to be heated, such as mini-bagels, soft pretzels, or pizza bites—to feed the whole group. Get an extra package, too. Keep the extra package frozen, but heat up the rest before the session. Put the frozen snacks and the heated ones on separate trays.

As the meeting starts, bring out just the frozen snacks and offer them to people. When they turn you down, act as if you don't know what the problem is. Pick up a frozen snack and gnaw on it, saying: **Mmm! You guys don't know what you're missing! How come nobody else wants any?**

When someone suggests that the snacks should be heated up, act amazed: **Huh? You mean you can heat these things up? What a concept!**

Now bring out the heated snacks. Say: **I guess temperature can make a big difference. It's easy to see that with food. But how about families? What happens when a family's emotional temperature is too cold or too hot?**

Listen to replies. Then say: **The authors of *The Heritage* believe the emotional environment in which we grow up is a major factor in shaping our futures. Here's a quote from their book:**

"If thoughts of your childhood bring fear rather than fondness, imagine what it would be like for family memories to warm your heart rather than tighten your stomach. Now imagine yourself giving such feelings to your own children. It is possible. And the first step is understanding what an emotional legacy should be, and can be."

At this point, pass out the heated snacks. As people eat, read the rest of the quote from *The Heritage*:

"A strong emotional legacy will give a child healthy emotions that allow him or her to deal in a positive way with the struggles of life.

Here's a definition of a strong emotional legacy: **A strong emotional legacy is that enduring sense of security and emotional stability, nurtured in an environment of safety and love."**

Repeat the definition. Then say: **When I offered you the frozen food, how could you tell it wasn't the right temperature?** (It had frost on it, there was no smell, etc.)

What clues might tell you whether a home had the right emotional temperature? What would that "environment of safety and love" look like?

Affirm replies. As needed, supplement group members' suggestions with these by the authors of *The Heritage*:

A Strong Emotional Legacy...
• Provides a safe environment in which deep emotional roots can grow.
• Fosters confidence through stability.
• Conveys a tone of trusting support.
• Nurtures a strong sense of positive identity.
• Creates a "resting place" for the soul.
• Demonstrates unconditional love.

A Weak Emotional Legacy...
• Breeds insecurity and shallow emotional development.
• Fosters fearfulness through instability.
• Conveys a tone of mistrust, criticism, or apathy.
• Undermines a healthy sense of personal worth.
• Causes inward turmoil.
• Communicates that a person doesn't measure up.

❷ Blueprint for Happiness

Objective:

To help group members discover biblical ingredients that make an emotionally healthy home (15-20 minutes).

How do we create the kind of environment that produces a strong emotional legacy? The Bible has some things to say about that.

Have group members turn to Colossians 3:12-14. **What "clothes" do we need to wear around the house?** (Compassion, kindness, humility, gentleness, patience, forgiveness, and love.)

Do you think it's easier to wear these "clothes" at work, at church, or at home? Why?

Imagine for a moment that this room has a giant thermometer on the wall. We'll call that end [point to one corner] **"Boiling Hot." We'll call that end** [point to other corner] **"Freezing Cold." I'm going to ask some questions, and you move to a spot along the "thermometer" to**

indicate your answers.

After each of the following questions, give people time to move to the places they choose. Answers will vary; as time allows, let volunteers explain their positions.

What might be the emotional temperature of a home that lacked compassion?

Of a home that lacked kindness?

Humility?

Gentleness?

Patience?

Forgiveness?

Love?

As needed, explain that in most cases temperatures could be at either extreme—depending on the personalities of family members. For example, a father who lacked compassion might be "chilly" toward his children—or "hot" with anger when they displeased him. A mother who lacked forgiveness might choose to "freeze out" those who wronged her—or explode with rage toward them. The point is that a home without these biblical qualities will be one of emotional turmoil, not one that promotes the security, stability, and safety needed for a strong emotional legacy.

After group members sit down, ask: **What quality seems to be most important in this passage?** (Love.) **Let's see how that quality might make a difference in a real-life home.**

Pass out copies of "Home Inspection" (RS-5A). Have participants work in groups of two or three. Remind the group that there are no "wrong answers" in this exercise, and group members may disagree over specific applications of the I Corinthians 13 principles. The important thing is to discover that biblical love is more than just a word; it has many facets, and each one has practical value in creating an emotionally healthy home.

After allowing time for small groups to work their way through several of the rooms on the handout, let volunteers share results with the whole group.

---

❸ Hit Parade

Objective:
To show how adults can help kids withstand emotional "hits" in order to preserve a healthy emotional legacy (15 minutes).

If you have time before the session, make an exotic-looking "machine" by combining some unrelated spare parts (such as a calculator, a can opener, and a yo-yo), or simply draw some scientific-looking dials on a cardboard box. Get ready to display your contraption during the following comments; if you don't make a machine, just make the comments.

There's a lot we can do to create a healthy emotional environment

at home. But what about the rest of the world? We can't guarantee that the children we love won't take an emotional "hit" on the playground, at a friend's house, or an after-school job. That's why you **need** [at this point hold up your "machine"] **the Wrongco Posterity Protector!**

Yes, the Wrongco Posterity Protector creates an invisible but impenetrable force field around the children you love. No longer will they be affected by taunts, abuse, or other trauma. You can rest easy in the knowledge that your emotional legacy will be preserved, thanks to Wrongco!

Unfortunately, this device has one tiny flaw. It doesn't work.

So how can we help children deal with the emotional "hits" they're bound to take in this fallen world? Listen to any ideas group members have.

The authors of *The Heritage* have some ideas, too. They suggest that giving a child a strong emotional legacy provides him or her with a "stabilizer bar" that helps the child withstand everyday emotional hits. When the stabilizer bar is damaged by trauma, they offer three steps for repairing it.

Pass out copies of "Just in Case" (RS-5B)-one copy to each of the small groups that were formed in Step 2. Call attention to the "Repairing the Stabilizer Bar" section of the sheet and have one person in each group read it to the others.

Now have the groups look at the case studies on the handout. Challenge them to apply the three steps to one or both of the cases, depending on how much time you have.

After a few minutes, share results. Supplement with the following ideas as needed.

Case One: The Girl Who Was Different

1. *Recognize and divert the impact of the pain.* Let Nicole talk about her feelings and don't minimize them. Rather than expecting her to adjust immediately, give her time. Make sure family members let her know that she's loved, and that her "difference" doesn't change their relationship with her.

2. *Repair the damage.* Tell the truth—that the situation may not change, that it's not her fault, that God cares and has good plans for her despite the hearing problem.

3. *Give the child a place of rest, not rescue.* Alternatives could be explored with a hearing specialist, but Nicole will have to learn to live with the loss. Find out all you can about helping her to do that.

Case Two: Lasting Impact

1. *Recognize and divert the impact of the pain.* Encourage Jeremy to talk about the accident and his feelings. Let him know he's accepted, even if he's afraid or angry.

2. *Repair the damage.* Tell the truth—that he's not a baby for being scared, that he won't always feel this way, that accidents happen but not that often, that even though God may not prevent an accident He can help us deal with it.

3. *Give the child a place of rest, not rescue.* Jeremy can't avoid cars for the rest of his life. Help him to feel as safe as you can—showing him you're driving carefully, bringing along other family members—and keeping the lines of communication open so that he can continue to express his fears as needed.

❹ Room for Improvement

Objective:

To help each person choose one way in which to improve the emotional environment of his or her home this week (5-10 minutes).

To wrap up the session, have small groups look at their blueprints from Step 2. Each person should respond to the following questions, sharing answers with others in the small group if he or she feels comfortable doing so.

Let's pretend this is a blueprint of your home. In which of these rooms do most of your family conflicts seem to occur?

Which of the I Corinthians 13 principles do you most need to apply in that room this week?

How could applying that principle help to build a stronger emotional legacy for the children you love?

After giving groups time to share their answers, close in prayer—asking God to help group members set the emotional thermostats of their homes to a healthy temperature this week.

Get Along, Little Dogie

6

Session Aim:

To help participants prepare children to "get along" in society by beginning to build them a healthy social legacy.

Billy had a weak spiritual legacy, which contributed to his anger and foul speech. But his appetite for stealing, brawling, and abusing his wife came directly from his lack of a solid social legacy. Neither his father nor his mother had any desire to build a relationship with their son.

Children must learn to relate to family members, peers, teachers, and eventually coworkers, the boss, customers, the banker, the butcher, and the baker. Like it or not, relating well to others is vital to the process of living. And for better or worse, the primary classroom of relational competence is the home, which is why it is so critical that we understand the importance of passing a solid relational legacy to our children.

Clearly, a strong social legacy is a great gift. And the strength of this legacy depends, as do the spiritual and emotional components, on our modeling as parents. Consider your own parents. If you grew up in a family that avoided conflict at all costs, you may become a doormat. If your parents tried to influence each other through shouting matches and manipulation, as an adult you may find yourself using similar approaches. Whatever the pattern may have been, it tends to show up in present and future relationships.

—*J. Otis Ledbetter and Kurt Bruner*

Getting Ready

Scriptures:

Matthew 19:17-19; 20:25-28;
Luke 6:31; Romans 12:16-19;
13:1.

1. Make four copies of the skit, "Fault Lines" (RS-6A). Choose people to play the parts. If possible, give them a chance to practice once before the session. Set up one chair for the witness stand, and a chair and table for the Judge. If you can provide the Judge with a gavel or rubber mallet, so much the better.
2. Bring Bibles, pencils, and enough paper for teams to take notes in Step 2.
3. Make copies of "Box Socials" (RS-6B), one for every two or three group members.
4. Ask a group member to bring a game with which most of your participants probably aren't familiar. Make sure you have the instructions. You'll also need a way to amplify your voice—like a battery-powered bullhorn or a piece of paper rolled into a cone-shaped megaphone.
5. Copy the reproducible resource you used in Session 2, "Social Legacy Evaluation" (RS-2C)—one copy per group member. You'll be using this sheet in a different way this time.

❶ Menace to Society

Objective:

To help each person see why it's important to leave kids a sound social heritage (5-10 minutes).

Have four volunteers perform the skit, "Fault Lines" (RS-6A). You may want to set the tone before and after the skit by having a group member hum the theme music from the old *Twilight Zone* TV show.

After the skit, lead a round of applause for your actors and discuss:

Have you ever wondered whether one of your kids might turn out to be a menace to society? If one did turn out that way, do you think people might blame you? Why or why not?

When you read or hear about a criminal in the news, especially a young one, do you make any assumptions about his or her parents? What thoughts about the criminal's upbringing tend to cross your mind?

What percentage of blame do you think the parents of a criminal deserve? Why?

What happens to a child who doesn't learn to relate well to others?

After considering replies, read the following quote from *The Heritage*:

"The most significant skill you can give your child is not academic prowess or business savvy. It is the fine art of relating to people. . . . Those who learn to relate well to others have an edge in the game of life. Those who don't are doomed to mediocrity at best, and failure at worst."

Invite volunteers to briefly agree or disagree before moving to Step 2.

❷ The Book of Virtues

Objective:
To help group members discover how God wants us to relate to each other, and to help them consider how these principles can be passed on to children (20-25 minutes).

Form groups of at least two or three persons each. Make sure each group has Bibles, a sheet of paper, and a pencil. Give the following instructions:

Congratulations! Your group has been chosen by the school board to come up with a public school curriculum that teaches kids how to behave in society. Your raw material, strangely enough, is a collection of Bible passages.

One person in each group should write down the following references as you read them: **Matthew 19:17-19; 20:25-28; Luke 6:31; Romans 12:16-19; 13:1.**

Since this is a public school curriculum, though, it can make no direct reference to Scripture. No quoting Bible verses. Simply list all the principles you can find in these passages that describe how people should relate to each other. Add any suggestions you might have for methods that could be used in teaching these principles. And remember—the final result must not sound as if it came from the Bible.

Give groups several minutes to work on this. Then share results. Principles might include the following, though they could be expressed in many ways:

Matthew 19:17-19—You have no right to take another person's life; once you're married, you shouldn't have sex with anyone but your spouse; don't take anything that belongs to someone else; don't tell a lie to get someone else in trouble; respect your parents; care about other people as much as you care about yourself.

Matthew 20:25-28—The highest honor you can have is to meet someone else's needs.

Luke 6:31—Treat others the way you'd like to be treated.

Romans 12:16-19—Do your best to get along with others; don't look down on anyone; don't try to get back at people.

Romans 13:1—Obey the laws, the school rules, and those who enforce them.

If groups came up with methods for teaching the principles, listen to those, too.

Then ask: **Do you think most kids learn these principles in school? At home? Anywhere?**

Have the children you love learned these principles? If not, will they? How?

Give each small group a copy of "Box Socials" (RS-6B). Call attention to the first box on the sheet.

The authors of *The Heritage* believe these are four building blocks for a solid social legacy. The first is respect. Who and what do you think children need to learn to respect? (God, oneself, peers, one's possessions, others' possessions, parents, other authorities, etc.)

The second building block is responsibility. How would you teach a child responsibility? (Give him or her duties around the house, etc.)

The third building block is love and acceptance. How would loving and accepting a child help him or her to get along as an adult? (The child would know how to love and accept others; the child would be less likely to seek love and acceptance in harmful ways.)

The fourth building block is borders—social boundaries that are not to be crossed. Can you think of borders you don't want the children you love to cross?

As needed, note that the authors of *The Heritage* list questions like the following that could be answered by establishing borders:

- How important is my tone of voice when I talk to my parents and others?
- Where do my rights end and the rights of others begin?
- Is it ever right to fight?
- How should I react when others are treated wrongly?

Now call attention to the second box on the sheet. Ask one group member to read aloud the traits of a strong social legacy. Then have another read the traits of a weak social legacy.

Ask: **How do you feel when you hear this list? Tired? Hopeful? Like it's too late? Like you have your work cut out for you?**
Let group members respond if they wish.

---

❸ Up Close and Personal

Objective:
To encourage participants to teach rules within the context of a loving relationship (10-15 minutes).

Building a strong social legacy isn't easy. But it goes a lot more smoothly if we keep an important principle in mind. We're about to see that principle at work.

During the week before the session, ask a group member to bring a game that probably isn't familiar to most in the group. At this point during the meeting, take the printed rules of the game and stand at a distance from the group. You'll need to amplify your voice with a battery-powered bullhorn, a microphone, or just a rolled-up paper megaphone.

Announce that the group is about to learn the rules of the game. Start reading the rules in a flat, monotonous tone. Stop after about 30 seconds. Ask: **Now do you understand how to play?** Most group members probably won't.

Say: **OK, let's try something else.** Have the person who brought the game gather the group around him or her. The person should show by example how to play the game, encouraging and answering questions along the way. After a few minutes, thank the person and have group members take their seats.

Which approach was more effective in teaching you how to play the game? Why? (The up-close-and-personal way, because it showed understanding of the difficulties people may have been having in learning the rules. It was also supported by example.)

Call attention to the last box on the "Box Socials" sheet. Have a volunteer read the "Rules within Relationship" section aloud. Ask: **When we tried to teach the group the rules of the game, which of us was more like Jason's parents? Why?** (You were; you were distant, apparently unfeeling, didn't allow questions, and didn't provide a model.)

How might remembering the "rules within relationship" principle make building a strong social legacy go more smoothly for you?

❹ Thanks for the Memories

Objective:
To help group members evaluate whether they need to strengthen their families' social rules, relationships, or both (10 minutes).

Give each person a copy of "Social Legacy Evaluation" (RS-2C). You probably used this handout in Session 2, when group members evaluated the legacies they've received. This time you want them to complete the form as their children might 20 years from now, based on the way group members have tried to teach their kids about relationships so far. (Note: Group members with no children at home should complete the form on behalf of children in their extended families.)

After people have completed and scored the evaluations, see whether anyone wants to comment or share results.

Then ask: **Based on your children's hypothetical responses to these questions, which do you need to work on more this week: rules or relationships? Do you need to be clearer about where the borders are? Or do you need to strengthen the relationship, be more up-close-and-personal in order to teach the rules more effectively?**

Participants may or may not wish to respond aloud. Say: **Pick one rule or relationship that needs to be reinforced with a child you love, and start reinforcing it this week.** If time permits, encourage people to re-form their small groups and pray for each other as they prepare to teach children about relationships this week.

Smells Like Team Spirit

7

Session Aim:

To motivate group members to create a loving environment at home by showing affection, encouraging respect, maintaining order, fostering merriment, and affirming each family member.

Christmas has its own spiciness, Thanksgiving its sweet bounty of fresh fruit pies, and each may remind us of special family gatherings. Family fragrances go deeper than the senses, however. They can have a lot to do with all three legacies—the emotional, spiritual, and social.

If you were asked to explain the aromatic definition of your family legacies—if you had to describe them as memories—what words would you select? Would it be the spicy scent from a healthy exchange of differing opinions, coupled with mutual respect? Or would it be a pungent odor from a home's chaotic, criticizing, and uncaring atmosphere?

There are five key qualities to a healthy family fragrance, each contributing to an environment of love in the home. We call them the Fragrance Five. It's easy to remember the Fragrance Five; we can fit them into an acrostic using the word Aroma: Affection, Respect, Order, Merriment, Affirmation.

Thus the first item from our heritage tool chest is a spice featuring five distinct fragrances that scent the home with love, creating an environment conducive to a positive heritage. Let's examine the contribution of each fragrance to a loving home.

—*J. Otis Ledbetter and Kurt Bruner*

Getting Ready

Scriptures:

Proverbs 10:12; 12:25; 15:13, 17; 16:24; 17:22; 19:26; 20:20; 27:5; I Timothy 3:4, 5, 12; 5:14; I Peter 2:12, 17.

1. Bring as many different kinds of room-scenting products as you can find (see Step 1) and set them on a table. Get a stick of deodorant to use as a prize, too.
2. Make sure you have a display surface (chalkboard and chalk, erasable marker board and marker, etc.) for Step 2. You'll also need Bibles.
3. Photocopy "Making Scents" (RS-7A) and cut apart the five scenes thereon. You'll need to copy and cut enough sheets so that you have one scene for every two group members.
4. Copy "Aromatic Actions" (RS-7B)—one copy per group member. Bring pencils, too.
5. If possible, bring a small, scented item to give each person or household as a reminder (see Step 4).

❶ Clearing the Air

Objective:

To help group members begin to consider what it means to have a "fragrant" home (10 minutes).

Before the session, collect a variety of room-scenting products (spray air freshener, plug-in, potpourri, pine-scented tree for hanging, scented candle, bottled room deodorizer, aromatic cedar, scented oil for a hurricane lamp, etc.). Display these on a table.

Ask for three volunteers to participate in a salesmanship contest. Each volunteer chooses one of the products on the table and tries to convince the group in 60 seconds that the chosen product is the best way to create a fragrant home.

Have your salespeople make their pitches; then vote to pick the best presentation. Give the winner a stick of deodorant as a prize.

Then ask the group: **What kind of scent do you like your home to have? Why?**

What smells do you remember fondly from the home in which you grew up? Have you tried to make your home smell that way?

What do you think is the best way to create a truly fragrant home?

As needed, point out that the answer depends on your definition of "fragrant." In this session you'll be defining that word in a rather unusual way.

❷ Sweet Smell of Success

Objective:

To help group members discover five "fragrances" that create an environment conducive to a positive heritage (15-20 minutes).

The authors of *The Heritage* use the word "fragrance" to describe the atmosphere of a home-its overall environment. The right family fragrance, they say, goes a long way toward building a solid heritage. They've identified five key qualities that create a healthy family fragrance-the Fragrance Five.

On a display surface (chalkboard, erasable board, posterboard, etc.), write the letters *AROMA* vertically.

The Fragrance Five are easy to remember, because their first letters spell the word "aroma." What do you suppose the Fragrance Five might be?

Invite a group member to come to the board and write his or her guesses. Others may call out suggestions. Results might be enlightening (Assurance, Reconciliation, Objectivity, Modeling, Acceptance) or amusing (Apple pie, Roast beef, Onions, Meatloaf, Asparagus).

Affirm any decent tries and thank the person for helping. Then write the following acrostic from *The Heritage:*

Affection
Respect
Order
Merriment
Affirmation

Let's see what the Bible has to say about these five qualities.

Write the following references on the board and assign individuals to look them up:

Affection—Proverbs 10:12; 15:17; 27:5.
Respect—Proverbs 19:26; 20:20; I Peter 2:12, 17.
Order—I Timothy 3:4, 5, 12; 5:14.
Merriment—Proverbs 15:13; 17:22.
Affirmation—Proverbs 12:25; 16:24.

Have the passages read aloud. After each reading, ask: **What does the passage say about the importance of this element of the Fragrance Five?** As needed, supplement replies with the following.

Affection
Proverbs 10:12—It neutralizes wrongs that could create a bad "odor."
15:17—It can make a lack of wealth easier to take.
27:5—It's vital to express it, not just to feel it.

Respect
19:26—A lack of it brings shame and disgrace.
20:20—Its opposite can be a serious crime (see Leviticus 20:9).
I Peter 2:12, 17—It attracts others to God.
Order
I Timothy 3:4, 5, 12—It's so basic that it's a requirement for certain kinds of church leadership.
5:14—It's for women, too, and helps the cause of Christ.
Merriment
Proverbs 15:13—It can greatly affect our mood and make us more pleasant to be around.
17:22—It may improve our physical health.
Affirmation
12:25—It can help lift depression and lighten things up.
16:24—It "tastes" good, and it's good for you.

Then ask: **If you had to assign an actual smell to each of these qualities, what would you choose? For example, would merriment smell like a Christmas tree because you associate that with the fun of opening presents? Would affection smell like your grandmother's perfume because of her hugs?**

Give group members a few moments to think about this; the process will help them begin to see how these five concepts might relate to real-life experiences. Listen to replies before moving to Step 3.

❸ AROMA Therapy

Objective:

To give participants the chance to practice incorporating the Fragrance Five into typical family situations (15-20 minutes).

Form pairs. Give each pair the instructions for role-playing a scene, cut from copies you've made of "Making Scents" (RS-7A). One person in each pair plays the parent; the other plays the child. Give pairs a couple of minutes to prepare; then have as many pairs as you have time for act out their scenes for the rest of the group.

Each scene should last no more than a minute. While each scene is being performed, the rest of the group may comment on the "fragrance" of what's going on by calling out "Ahhh!" for good "smells" and "Phew!" for bad ones. Be sure to explain that these are comments on the qualities the characters are displaying, not reviews of the performances.

After each scene, challenge the whole group to suggest ways in which the parent could use some of the Fragrance Five to handle the conflict in a "sweet-smelling" way. Here are ideas to use as needed:

Scene One: Affection

The parent should feel free to express affection, but in ways the child will perceive as affection. This is a way of respecting and affirming the child's desire to be "grown up." If a kiss at the school door doesn't work anymore, why not try something else? A kiss or hug might still be accepted further from school and closer to home. The parent might also defuse the conflict through merriment, making a good-natured joke about the problem or trying some tickles instead of a kiss.

Scene Two: Respect

The parent needs to bring order to the home by discussing and setting boundaries—including the boundary around the child's room, which the parent should respect. The parent could also affirm the child's apparent rejection of drugs so far. And before delivering more antidrug lectures, the parent could make sure to cultivate the kind of affectionate relationship with the child that provides a positive context for laying down rules.

Scene Three: Order

Bringing order out of chaos should be the parent's priority. Much of the problem might be solved by establishing an evening routine of preparing for the next morning. The parent could show respect by inviting the child to help plan the preparation process, and by giving the child significant responsibility for getting ready. Showing affection may be in order when something like a bad dream interrupts the routine; a little merriment could be injected to lighten the busy morning, perhaps in the form of a riddle at wake-up time.

Scene Four: Merriment

Playing along with the jokes would be a way to express affection in this situation. It would also affirm the child's ability to remember and tell a joke, as well as his/her sense of humor. The stressed-out parent understandably sees the need for order, especially after a chaotic day. Postponing the jokes for a little while might help. But merriment might be the best medicine for both parent and child.

Scene Five: Affirmation

Overt expressions of affection or merriment probably wouldn't be accepted by the child yet. The parent needs to show respect by giving the child time to calm down. After that happens, the parent could seek to bring order to the situation by helping to put the experience in perspective—perhaps relating a similar experience from his or her childhood or comparing the importance of this contest to that of other tests to come. The parent can affirm the child's ambition, industry, and interest in science without reinforcing his/her perfectionism.

❹ Personal Hygiene

Objective:

To help group members choose specific ways to improve the "fragrances" of their homes this week (5-10 minutes).

Pass out copies of "Aromatic Actions" (RS7-B), one to each person, along with pencils. Let group members get a chuckle from the tongue-in-cheek multiple choices on the sheet before asking them to write in their own plan for what they can do in each area this week.

Emphasize that these action plans don't need to turn the world upside down; they just need to be specific and workable. Note that the more modest the plans are, the more likely people will be to follow through.

If possible, close the session by giving each group member (or household) a scented item as a reminder of the Fragrance Five. This might be a scratch 'n' sniff sticker, a small bar of scented soap, a small package of potpourri, a stick of incense, or a scented votive candle. Encourage people to put these items in a prominent place at home to help them remember the usefulness of family fragrance in the heritage-building process.

8 Tradition!

Session Aim:

To help group members use existing family traditions in building a heritage, and to help them create new traditions for this purpose as needed.

There is a place for leaving home—physically and emotionally—and becoming our own person. But there is also a place for building and maintaining a strong sense of identity by passing on a traditional understanding of who we are, and where we have come from. We are too quick to break from that heritage in the name of individualism.

We are not suggesting that all tradition is good. Some traditions can actually undermine a healthy sense of identity. But our generation seems to have burned down the house to get rid of the roaches. Instilling an appreciation of who we are, where we have come from, and how we should live is a vital part of family life. Unfortunately, all too often, it is the part of family life we neglect. We've cut ourselves off from our roots—leaving nothing to nourish our wavering sense of identity.

Our goal is to renew your sense of appreciation for the role of tradition in family life. Not a dry, empty ritual. But fresh, meaningful activities which undergird the process of passing an emotional, spiritual, and relational inheritance between generations. As we will see, family tradition can play a vital role in that process.

—*J. Otis Ledbetter and Kurt Bruner*

Getting Ready

Scriptures:

Psalm 48

1. Cue a "Fiddler on the Roof" videotape to the opening sequence that leads to the song "Tradition." If possible, have a group member bring a short (no more than two minutes) home video of a humorous family event. Make sure you have a TV ready, and a VCR that can play the tape (or have the group member bring his or her camcorder with a direct-to-TV hookup). Bring a prize for the winner of the Step 1 contest, too.
2. Find two tapes or CDs—one containing music that appeals to young children and one featuring music popular with teenagers (enlist the help of group members if you're not up on these age groups' current tastes). Choose from each album a song that tells a story (see Step 3). Have a tape player or CD player ready.
3. Bring Bibles, pencils, and paper.
4. Make copies of "Days of Our Lives" (RS-8A) and "Take It on Home" (RS-8B). You'll need one copy of each sheet for each household represented in the group.

❶ Funniest Home Videos

Objective:

To encourage participants to consider the role that family history already plays in their lives (5-10 minutes).

Open the session by showing the opening section of the video "Fiddler on the Roof" through the song "Tradition." **Family history is formed by tradition and memories. What are some of yours?**

If possible, have a group member bring a short (two minutes or less) home video of a humorous family event—a child falling asleep in a plate of spaghetti, family members trying to extricate Dad from under the sink, etc. Start the session by showing the video. Then ask the person who brought it what the significance of that event has been for the family. Do family members still talk about it? Will they want to see that tape in 20 years? Why or why not?

Whether or not you begin with a video, hold a "Funniest Home Video That Got Away" contest for the whole group at this point. Invite volunteers to tell stories of things that happened in their families that *would* have made good videos if only they'd been taping.

After hearing a few stories, let the group vote on the best. Give the winner a small prize—perhaps a toy camera for capturing those future family events.

Then ask: **Let's say that tomorrow when you wake up, no one in your family can remember anything that's happened before today. The memories, the traditions, the in jokes, the pet names-all are gone. How might that affect your family?** (Our identity would be lost; we wouldn't have as much to hold us together, etc.)

If that happened, what would you do? (We'd have to create new traditions, start over, etc.)

❷ Traditional Values

Objective:
To help group members discover how using events, stories, and creeds can help build a solid heritage (15-20 minutes).

The authors of *The Heritage* know the value of family tradition and family history. In fact, they believe tradition is one of the most important tools for building a heritage. Here's how they define tradition:

"**Tradition: The practice of handing down stories, beliefs, and customs from one generation to another in order to establish and reinforce a strong sense of identity.**"

They further define tradition by breaking it down into three areas: events, stories, and creed.

Ask participants to turn to Psalm 48. Have several group members read it aloud, a few verses at a time.

Ask: **What events does the psalmist mention?** (God's help when enemy nations joined forces and attacked, only to retreat in terror when they saw that Zion was the city of the Great King. This sounds much like events that occurred in the days of Jehoshaphat [II Chronicles 20] and Hezekiah [II Kings 19:35-36].)

How does that help to pass along a heritage? (It reinforces the identity of God's people as a chosen nation and motivates them to serve Him, even if they weren't around when the events happened.)

Now take another look at the psalm. How does the story told in this psalm differ from the way a newspaper report might be written? (A newspaper report might give the facts, but this story delivers the facts with drama that emphasizes the enemies' fear and the power of God that left them "shattered.")

Why does the psalmist tell the story this way? (Because he's a "cheerleader" for God and His people; to make it clear that God is all-powerful and protects His people.)

Now take a third look at the psalm. Is there anything here that might be seen as a creed, a statement of belief? (Possibly verses 1-3, but especially verse 14.)

How is this creed supported by the story? (God protected His people as He said He would; His people in turn will be loyal to Him.)

Which do you think most families are best at today: events, stories, or creeds? Why?

Do you think most Christian families use tradition to reinforce biblical truths, or for other purposes?

Supplement responses with the following quote from *The Heritage*:

"**There is value in establishing certain traditions just for the sake of spending time together as a family. But there should also be traditions created that reinforce truth in the lives of our children. Traditions should serve to help our children fulfill Deuteronomy 6:5: 'Love the Lord your God with all your heart and with all your soul and with all your strength.'**"

❸ Keeping Up with the Joneses

Objective:

To help group members brainstorm ways to make events, stories, and creeds part of family life (15-20 minutes).

Form three teams—the Event Experts, the Story Squad, and the Creed Committee. Have them assemble in different areas of your meeting place. Give each team a pencil and a sheet of paper for taking notes.

Tell the Event Experts: **You're going to help out the Jones family down the street. The Joneses moved into this neighborhood exactly a year ago. It was a tough move, leaving their friends a thousand miles away. And it's been a tough year in some ways, with daughter Keesha getting over hepatitis and son Michael breaking up with his girlfriend. But they have a lot to celebrate. Your job is to figure out how they should do it. Plan a party that reminds them of how God has brought them through. You can spend up to $50.**

Give the Story Squad two tapes or CDs you've brought, along with the equipment to play them. On the first album should be a song that appeals to young children; on the second should be a song a teenager might like. Both songs should tell a story in some way. Tell the team: **These songs are from the Jones family down the street. The first is a favorite of little Keesha. The second is one teenager Michael likes. Each song contains a story. Listen carefully to the two songs; then answer these questions: (1) What do these songs tell you about Keesha and Michael—what moves them, motivates them, and concerns them? (2) How could the Joneses use musical stories like these to build a heritage for Keesha and Michael?**

Tell the Creed Committee: **The Joneses are a Christian family down the street. They have two children—Keesha, age six, and Michael, age 14. They need your help in writing a family creed. Your job is to make a list of at least 12 subjects the Joneses might want to address in their creed. Then organize them in order of importance. The Joneses will take it from there.**

Give teams several minutes to complete their tasks. If you have extra time, rotate the teams so that everyone will get a crack at each of the three tradition areas.

Have each team share its results and discoveries with the others. Encourage group members to listen for ideas they could apply to their own families—not just to the Joneses.

❹ We've Always Done It That Way

Objective:

To help participants choose their own family traditions to use in passing on a heritage (10 minutes).

Pass out copies of "Days of Our Lives" (RS-8A), one to each household represented. Members of each household should come up with one activity for each day of the week and categorize it according to the instructions on the sheet.

This handout asks you to identify your family traditions. Remember that traditions don't always involve a lot of fanfare. They can be simple. Here are a few examples that might already be traditions in your family:

- **Dad cooks breakfast one day a week.**
- **Play time with the kids when you come home from work.**
- **Parent/Child date nights.**
- **Choosing a family video together for Family Night.**

When participants have finished all or most of the exercise, let volunteers share results. Pay special attention to traditions that could be used to teach spiritual truths. Let people suggest to each other ways in which those traditions could be used for that purpose.

To close, distribute copies of "Take It on Home" (RS-8B), one per household. Encourage group members to complete this self-evaluation and planner when they have time during the week.

You Line Up My Life

9

Session Aim:

To help participants identify the standards of right and wrong that they want to pass on to the children they love.

Wilber, a friend who sets tiles, once explained how he keeps those tiny tiles in a straight line. After finding a level line near the floor, he uses a piece of equipment called a ninety-degree angle. With this right angle he can draw a truly vertical plumb line on the wall; everything in that room is measured by its standard.

"One time I tried to eyeball it," he said with a grin. "All the way up the wall, it looked right to me until I was about two-thirds done. I stood back and was horrified. It was so far off. The more I worked up the wall, the farther off the angle I got. In the midst of the task, it didn't seem wrong. But it was, and it cost me a great deal. I had to redo the entire job!"

We need a right angle, a tool in our heritage chest that lets us draw an accurate vertical line to show our children what is right. The right angle will keep our children on track, showing them what is normal, healthy living. Just as a tiler can't set each tile on the wall at its own angle and expect the finished product to look as it should, our children cannot have a healthy, accurate perspective on life without a straight plumb, which comes by having a true right angle measure.

—J. Otis Ledbetter and Kurt Bruner

Getting Ready

Scriptures:

Psalm 8:4-8; Proverbs 3:1-2, 5-8; 13:11; Matthew 6:31-33; 18:1-6; Ephesians 5:22-6:4; II Thessalonians 3:10-13; Hebrews 13:4.

1. Make sure you have a display surface (chalkboard and at least three pieces of chalk, or erasable marker board and markers, etc.) for the Step 1 contest. You'll also need a protractor, a device for measuring angles. Inexpensive plastic protractors are available in the school supplies section of many stores. Bring small prizes (mini-boxes of raisins, sticks of gum, etc.) for the winners.
2. Bring Bibles, pencils, and paper.
3. Make copies of "Plumb Lines" (RS-9A), one for every two group members.
4. Depending on which option you use in Step 4, either make copies of "Sign Here" (RS 9B)—one copy per group member-or make large posterboard versions of the road signs shown on the sheet. If you make the cardboard signs, bring poster tape, poster putty, or other means to attach them to the wall.

❶ Touched by an Angle

Objective:

To help each person see the need to communicate clear, objective standards of right and wrong to children (5-10 minutes).

Start with the following contest.

Choose three people to come to the front of the room and stand at the chalkboard, erasable marker board, or other display surface. Give each person a piece of chalk or marker, depending on the kind of board you're using. Then issue this challenge:

You have 15 seconds to draw a 45-degree angle. The person to come closest to 45 degrees doesn't win anything. The angle has to be *exactly* **45 degrees. Go!**

Let contestants try. Then measure the results with a protractor. If anyone has drawn the angle precisely (not likely), award him or her a small prize.

Repeat the process a few times with other contestants and other angles—anything between 10 degrees and 170 degrees.

After thanking contestants, ask the group: **Why was it so hard to draw the angle exactly?** (There was no objective standard to measure against.) **What would have made this easier?** (A protractor and a ruler.)

Let's say a child is helping you put up wallpaper in his or her room—a nightmare to contemplate, perhaps, but let's say you're doing it anyway. You tell the child, "We need to make sure this wallpaper will be straight. Go make a line on the wall at exactly a 90% angle to the floor." All you give the child is a pencil. What happens? (The line isn't drawn at the correct angle and the wallpaper goes up crooked.)

Now let's say your child comes to you with a problem. He or she wants to go to a party where the parents won't be home and three

kegs of beer will be tapped. All you say to the child is, "Do what you want." What happens? (If this is all you've ever told the child about what's right and wrong regarding drinking, he or she probably won't make the right choice.)

Most parents wouldn't expect their children to draw a right angle without the proper tools. But many parents seem to think their kids don't need tools to make the right moral choices. Today we're going to find out how to make sure our kids don't go off without their moral protractors.

❷ Right Angles

Objective:
To help group members identify key areas in which kids need clear standards of what's normal and what isn't (15 minutes).

When it comes to right angles, the authors of *The Heritage* have their own definition:

"For a strong heritage, we define the right angle this way: The right angle is the standard of normal, healthy living against which our children will be able to measure their attitudes, actions, and beliefs."

So who defines what's normal and abnormal, right and wrong? Listen to replies. Then ask a volunteer to read Proverbs 3:1-2, 5-8.

Who sets the right angle? (The Lord.)

Why can't we just lean on our own understanding? (We're not perfect.)

Why can't we just let our kids lean on theirs? (They're not perfect, either.)

How many moral choices do you suppose a child will face in his or her life? (Probably thousands.)

The authors of *The Heritage* have suggested these seven areas in which we need to pass along a right angle to the children we love. They offer these as several of many areas you might address.

On the chalkboard or other display surface, write the following:

SELF-WORTH
PERSONAL RESPONSIBILITY
DELAYED GRATIFICATION
SPIRITUAL EXPLORATION
PRIORITIES
SEXUALITY
FAMILY RESPONSIBILITIES

Which of these areas do you most feel the need to discuss today?

Which do you hope we don't get around to discussing? (Probably sexuality or spiritual exploration.)

Let's see if we can get to all these areas without blushing or having a fight break out.

Distribute copies of "Plumb Lines" (RS-9A). Have people work in pairs to discover the biblical norms and compare them with society's standards.

Then ask the whole group: **What biblical norms did you find here?** As needed, supplement replies with the following ideas.

Self-worth (Psalm 8:4-8)—Each person is created by God, just a little lower than created heavenly beings, crowned with glory and honor, managing other parts of God's creation.

Personal Responsibility (II Thessalonians 3:10-13)—People are to provide for themselves, earning the food they eat, rather than being idle.

Delayed Gratification (Proverbs 13:11)—Instead of trying to get rich quick through dishonesty, we should save a little at a time.

Spiritual Exploration (Matthew 18:1-6)—Children have the potential to please God; we must not discourage their faith or cause them to sin.

Priorities (Matthew 6:31-33)—Our first priority should be serving God and becoming holy; if we do this, other needs will be taken care of as well.

Sexuality (Hebrews 13:4)—We must take marriage very seriously, and limit sexual relations to marriage.

Family Responsibilities (Ephesians 5:22-6:4)—Wives and husbands are not the same. Wives are called to adaptive love and husbands are called to sacrificial love in a mutual relationship. You may want to note that evangelical scholars' interpretations differ when it comes to defining exactly what it means to be the "head" of the wife or to "submit" to the husband. How children and parents relate to one another is a crucial element in developing the "right angle," too.

Then ask: **How far off do you think society's standards are in these areas?** Opinions may vary widely; there's no need to reach consensus on this question. Instead, emphasize simply that we can't always rely on prevailing community standards to give our children a biblical "right angle."

❸ Secret Ballot

Objective:
To help participants clarify their views on some "right angle" issues and admit their difficulties in addressing those issues (15-20 minutes).

Pass out pencils and paper. You're going to take a survey, and people are going to respond by secret ballot.

Please number your paper from 1 to 14. I'm going to read a list of 14 actions. If you think the action is right, put an R after the number. If you think it's wrong, put a W. If you think it's neither right nor wrong, put an N. Then, if you would find it easy to talk about that action with your children, write an E. If you'd find it hard, write an H. You should end up with two letters after each number—RE, RH, WE, WH, NE, or NH.

Read the following list aloud, pausing after each action to allow people to write down the appropriate letters.

1. **Getting a tattoo of an eagle on your shoulder when you're 17 years old.**
2. **Refusing to go swimming at summer camp because people might see the purple birthmark on your leg.**
3. **Watching a TV show when it might be your only chance to do your homework.**
4. **Not marrying your girlfriend after you get her pregnant.**
5. **Taking out a loan to buy a new set of living room furniture instead of putting up with the old furniture for three more years and saving up the money.**
6. **Eating all your Halloween candy the first night, even if it gives you a stomach ache.**
7. **Skipping church because you think it's boring.**
8. **Dating someone who isn't a Christian.**
9. **Using your money to buy a new baseball card instead of contributing to a flood victims' relief fund.**
10. **Going to your best friend's birthday party even though you'd already promised to babysit the neighbor's child at that time.**
11. **Watching an R-rated movie on cable TV with a fellow 12-year-old.**
12. **Living together after you're engaged but before you're married.**
13. **Using your mom's makeup or your dad's tools without their permission.**
14. **Throwing a plate at your wife during an argument.**

Ask a couple of group members to collect the ballots and tally the results. While they're working on that, let volunteers react to the survey.

Were many of the choices tough? Why or why not?

What biblical principles led you to your responses?

How would you let your children know the Bible influenced your responses?

Which issues would be hardest to discuss with kids? Why?

What suggestions can you offer the rest of the group on addressing tough or embarrassing issues with kids?

As needed, supplement replies with these ideas from *The Heritage*:

- Take your son or daughter to dinner or on a weekend outing with the specific goal of addressing right and wrong sexual behavior.
- Recognize sexual differences by celebrating "Becoming a Woman Day" or "Becoming a Man Day" when the physical changes of puberty become apparent.

- Prepare a written contract in which the child agrees to undertake or avoid a particular behavior and you agree to offer your help and unconditional love.
- Be alert to questions that give you an opportunity to discuss a subject. For instance, a child might ask, "Where does God live?" or "Why did Grandpa die?"

When the survey results are tallied, have your volunteers announce the results. Are there any surprises? Chances are that right-and-wrong judgments weren't unanimous; rather than debating the issues, encourage group members to measure their responses against biblical standards, and to ask other mature believers for help when they aren't sure where to stand on questions to which children need answers.

❹ On the Road Again

Objective:
To encourage group members to address one "right angle" issue this week with the children they love (10-15 minutes).

In this step you'll be using road signs as symbols of right-angle messages that could be communicated to kids. The signs are printed for you on "Sign Here" (RS-9B). You may simply pass out copies of the sheet to group members; but if you have time during the week before the session, you could make larger, cardboard versions of the signs and post them on the walls of your meeting place. Use the art on the sheet as a reference for your signmaking.

If you use the reproducible sheet, distribute copies at this point. Have people look it over.

If you make larger signs for the walls, call attention to them now.

Ask: **Which of these signs is most like a "right angle" message you'd like to communicate this week to one of the children you love? For example, do you want the child to "Stop" something? Do you want to warn him or her about a hazard ahead? Do you want the child to "Rest" in the knowledge that his or her worth comes from God? Do you want the child to "Obey Your Signal Only" instead of listening to peers on a certain issue?**

If you're using the sheet, have participants circle the sign that's most like the message they'll communicate this week. If your signs are on the wall, have group members get up and stand by the signs of their choice.

In either case, encourage (but don't press) people to talk about the signs they've chosen.

Close by praying that group members will have the insight and strength they'll need this week to address these right-angle issues with the children they love.

Making an Impression

10

Session Aim:

To help participants understand the benefits and process of using verbal, symbolic, visual, and written impression points to build a heritage.

Jim and Janet watch their three children decorate the plastic-covered table. In drips and drabs, the toothpaste spreads across the tabletop; the three young kids are having the time of their lives squeezing the paste out of the tube. Jim watches closely, a smile ever-present. It's all part of his plan.

"OK," Dad says, slapping a twenty-dollar bill onto the table. "The first person to get the toothpaste back into their tube gets this money!" Little hands begin working; they have very little success, of course. "We can't do it, Dad!" protests the youngest child.

"The Bible tells us that's just like your tongue," Dad answers. "Once the words come out, it's impossible to get them back in. So be careful what you say because you may wish you could take it back." The children look at Dad and each other and smile. An unforgettable impression is made.

Not all impression points come by planning. Some of the best occur when our children do something unexpected and we respond. Had Jim stumbled on the children smearing the toothpaste without his permission, he had a teachable moment in the offing. He could then yell at them, or he could use their mess as an object lesson—to create an impression point.

—*J. Otis Ledbetter and Kurt Bruner*

Getting Ready

Scriptures:

Deuteronomy 6:6-9; Luke 22:14-20; John 13:1-17; 15:1-17; I John 2:1-14.

1. Bring pencils, paper, and Bibles.
2. Make copies of "How NOT to Make a Spiritual Impression on Your Kids" (RS-10A), one for every two group members; make four copies of "R.S.V.P." (RS-10B).
3. For each group member, bring a 3" x 5" index card, an envelope, and a postage stamp.

---

❶ Multimedia Museum

Objective:

To help group members discover the variety of ways in which a positive impression can be made on a child (10 minutes).

After greeting the group, ask: **Have you ever been to a children's museum? What was it like?**

As needed, note that it's usually a hands-on experience. Most exhibits are designed to be touched, cranked, crawled through, smelled, switched on, or otherwise used interactively. Computers may be featured, as well as video and other kinds of media.

Today we're going to design a new kind of children's museum—a Christian children's museum. The purpose of this place will be to impart biblical truths to kids, using as many methods as possible.

Form teams of two to four people each. Give each team a pencil and paper. **There are no budgetary limits on this project. You can build a facility as big as you like, and use anything from flannelgraph to robots. Go wild!**

Give teams a few minutes to come up with ideas. Then have them share results with the whole group. Affirm as many ideas as you can.

Then ask: **Which of these ideas could we adapt for use at home?** Chances are that many of the concepts could be scaled down for family use.

If only we could turn our homes into Christian children's museums, where kids would get a wide variety of experiences that made the right kind of impressions on them. What a great tool for heritage building that would be.

Come to think of it, maybe we can do just that.

---

❷ Master Teachers

Objective:

To show participants how Jesus and John used a variety of methods to make their points (15-20 minutes).

Children's museums are good at using a variety of methods to make an impression on kids. But they didn't invent the concept.

Have people turn to Deuteronomy 6:6-9. After a volunteer reads it aloud, ask: **How were parents to impress God's commandments on their children?** (By talking about them, using visual symbols, and writing them down.)

The authors of *The Heritage* call these teaching times "impression points." Listen to what they have to say:

"Impression points are those times in life when we make an impression upon others—when we 'impress' them with who we are, what we think, or what we do. The impressions may come to our children through our words, but impression points contain more power and lasting effect when they come through instructive events our children can observe. Impression points can be intentionally created, or they can incidentally occur. Either way, they make an impression… for good or bad."

The authors identify four kinds of impression points: verbal, symbolic, visual, and written. To understand how these work, let's look at some examples.

Divide the group into four teams. Assign the first team to read John 15:1-17.

The second team should read Luke 22:14-20.

The third team reads John 13:1-17.

The fourth team reads I John 2:1-4.

Tell all four teams: **After you read your passage, decide which type of impression point was used—verbal, symbolic, visual, or written.**

Share results. They should be something like this:

John 15:1-17—Verbal; Jesus talks to His disciples at a critical time. (Of course, here Jesus also used a word picture.) Some may point out that since this is a written record we're reading, it's a written impression point for us. That applies to all the passages.

Luke 22:14-20—The way Jesus used the cup and bread was symbolic. It was visual, too, not to mention using the senses of taste and touch. His explanation of the symbolism was verbal.

John 13:1-17—Mainly visual, though some might call it symbolic, too. There is a verbal element as Jesus explains his action.

I John 2:1-14—Written.

Why do you suppose Jesus used different kinds of impression points? Why not just deliver one sermon after another? (Probably because people learn in a variety of ways.)

Do you think most Christian families are good at using a variety of impression points in building a heritage? Why or why not? Opinions will vary. You may want to point out, though, that it's easy to get stuck in a rut—always reading from a devotional book, for example, or always having a conversation about God in the car after church.

Let's see how we can use a variety of impression points to build a heritage for the children we love.

❸ My Way

Objective:

To teach group members how to use verbal, symbolic, visual, and written impression points (15-20 minutes).

Have group members stay in their four teams during this step.

Pass out copies of "How NOT to Make a Spiritual Impression on Your Kids" (RS-10A), one for every two group members. Give people a couple of minutes to enjoy the cartoons.

Ask: **What kind of impression are you likely to make with these methods?** (A negative one.)

Let's try a more positive approach. Give each of the four teams a copy of "R.S.V.P." (RS-10B). Designate one team as Verbal, one as Symbolic, one as Visual, and one as Written. Each team should read the situations and respond to each with an impression point that fits its designation.

After allowing several minutes for teams to work their way through the sheet, discuss results. As needed, supplement suggestions with the following ideas—which are by no means exhaustive.

1. *Verbal response*—Read passages from Revelation describing activities in heaven and ask which of these things your daughter thinks Amy would like best.

Symbolic response—Have your daughter stand far away from you, then have her run into your arms and lift her up as high as you can. Ask whether she felt happier when she stood far away or when she finally reached you. In the same way, Amy is happy now because she's finally close to her heavenly Father.

Visual response—Look with your daughter at pictures of Amy in a family album, remembering things she liked to do and how she looked when she was especially happy. You could explain that Amy is at least that happy now, because she's doing things that God knows are the very best for her.

Written response—Write your daughter a poem describing things you think a person might do in heaven, or make a card expressing how you miss your sister but know you'll get to see her someday and ask her about all the things she's been doing.

2. *Verbal response*—Practice saying the books in order at the breakfast table.

Symbolic response—Come up with a simple picture that stands for each book of the Bible (a gavel for Judges, a musical note for Psalms, etc.) and use it as a memory aid.

Visual response—Draw visual symbols for the books on a long piece of paper and put it up as a border in your son's room.

Written response—Write a song that lists the books in order.

3. *Verbal response*—Take your son out for a walk and talk with him about the problem.

Symbolic response—Ask your son to join you for a snack; take bits of food from the garbage can and put them on your plates. When he protests, discuss how feeding our minds pornography is like feeding our bodies trash.

Visual response—Tape a picture of two eyes at the top of the computer monitor, along with a verse like "I will set before my eyes no vile thing" (Ps. 101:3).

Written response—Write your son a note about what you found in the garbage; later you might draw up a written contract between the two of you regarding use of the computer.

4. *Verbal response*—Explain that when we say Jesus lives in our hearts, we mean He's a special part of our lives. A friend, a parent, or even a country can be a special part of our lives without having to fit inside of us.

Symbolic response—Put a small picture of your daughter in a cameo necklace and wear it for a while. Then show it to her and explain that even though she's big, the tiny picture represents her. Wearing the cameo is a way of keeping her "close to your heart." Having Jesus "in your heart" is a way of saying He is always close to you.

Visual response—Make a giant heart-shaped valentine for your daughter. Use it to explain that your love for her is much bigger than your physical heart. Our love for Jesus can be big enough for Him to be "in" it.

Written response—Write a story about a girl who wants to keep all her friends close to her, so she tries to fit them in her closet. She discovers that they don't have to stay in her closet to be close friends. Read the story to your daughter and explain how this is like staying close to Jesus without actually trying to fit Him in our physical hearts.

Ask: **Which kind of impression points do you think will come most naturally to you?**

Which kind do you think the children you love will respond to best? Encourage group members to experiment with a variety of impression points in the coming weeks, to see which work best for them.

❹ Mail Bonding

Objective:

To give each person the chance to use one kind of impression point right now (5-10 minutes).

Give each group member a 3" x 5" index card, an envelope, and a postage stamp.

In the time that remains, try creating a written impression point for a child you love. Write him or her a note—thanking the child for a good thing he or she did recently, or encouraging the child as he or she faces a tough situation at school or elsewhere. If your child can't read yet, don't worry—you can read the note to him or her when it arrives in the mail. I'll gather these notes in a few minutes, and drop them in the mailbox today so the children you're writing will receive them sometime this week.

Allow time for people to write their notes. Have them put the notes in the envelopes, which they should address and stamp. Collect these for mailing.

Close by praying that God will use these written impression points to help build a strong heritage for the children to whom they're addressed.

Here's the Plan

11-13

Session Aim:

To help group members create specific plans for applying what they've learned about building a heritage.

Let's face it. The chief reason many of us fail to give a solid heritage is not lack of desire, incompetence, or even the baggage from our past. The number one reason we fail to give a solid heritage is negligence—we neglect to create a plan for doing so. The typical family reacts to the daily events of life, instead of intentionally planning the heritage-passing process. So they find themselves ricocheting through daily family life, bouncing here and there.

Big mistake!

As the Japanese proverb puts it, "When you're dying of thirst, it's too late to think about digging a well." Sadly, many parents don't even think about the impact of their heritage process until it is too late.

We believe anyone can give a strong heritage. But doing so requires a plan. Everything you've studied so far has been preparation for these three sessions.

Of course, once the plan is created, it must be carried out. But experience tells us that those who write down a plan are much more likely to get it done.

—J. Otis Ledbetter and Kurt Bruner

Getting Ready

Scriptures:

Matthew 7:7-11; Philippians 1:4-6; 4:4-9, 13.

Note: This session plan is actually three meetings in one. Sessions 11-13 are times for your group members to work as individuals, couples, or small groups to plan how they'll carry out what they've learned about building a heritage. All three "workshop" sessions follow the same format: Greet the group and give instructions; encourage people with Scripture and let them choose the reproducible sheets they'd like to work on; allow time for people to work through the sheets they've chosen; then let people share ideas, successes, and concerns, and let them pray for each other.

1. Bring Bibles, pencils, and paper.
2. Prepare refreshments if you like.
3. Choose the Bible passage (see Step 2) you'd like to use for encouraging group members.
4. Make copies of the 10 reproducible sheets available for these final three sessions: "Planning Your Heritage: Getting Started" (RS-11-13A); "Family Fragrance Factory" (RS-11-13B); "Impression Point Pointers" (RS-11-13C); "Right Angle Workshop" (RS-11-13D); "Writing Your Family Creed" (RS-11-13E); "Family Traditions Calendar" (RS-11-13F); "Marking Your Milestones" (RS-11-13G); "Family Night Planner" (RS-11-13H); "Leading a Child to Christ, Part I" (RS-11-13I); "Leading a Child to Christ, Part II" (RS-11-13J). Put the sheets in stacks on a table in your meeting place, smorgasbord style, so group members can look them over and pick the ones they want. Make enough copies of each sheet so that each household represented can have one. Check your supply after Sessions 11 and 12 to make sure you have enough.

❶ Your World and Welcome to It

Objective:

To help group members focus on the task of applying what they've learned about building a heritage (5 minutes).

Make refreshments available if you like. Greet the group and open the meeting with prayer, asking God to help all of you plan how you'll use what you've learned to build a heritage.

Explain that in these final three sessions, you're going boldly where you haven't been before: beyond theory and into planning specifically how each household represented will build the heritage you've been talking about.

Explain that in a few moments participants will get to look over the worksheets you've brought, and to choose the ones that interest them most. People can tackle the sheets in any order they like, though it would be a good idea to begin with "Planning Your Heritage: Getting Started" (RS-11-13A). Group members are free to work as individuals, couples, or in small groups. They should work at their own speed; it's unlikely that they'll finish all the worksheets in three sessions. They can feel free to take sheets home to work on, too.

❷ Thought for The Day

Objective:

To encourage participants with the knowledge that God can produce life-changing results from the plans they make during this session (5 minutes).

Choose one of the following passages to read aloud to the group. Your purpose is to encourage participants briefly as they face the task of applying what they've learned. Questions and comments for each passage are provided.

Matthew 7:7-11

Based on this passage, would you say God understands your desire to build a strong heritage for the children you love? Why or why not? (Yes; He's a father, and knows that we want to give good things to our children despite our flaws.)

How could these verses encourage you as you start the task of planning your heritage? (God stands ready to help us with this process if we ask Him; He wants to give us good gifts.)

Philippians 1:4-6

Who was building a heritage here? (Paul; he was passing on a heritage to the Philippians.)

Why was he so upbeat about how things were going to turn out? (He was impressed by the enthusiasm the Philippians had shown from the start, and their willingness to be partners in the process. But Paul's confidence really lay in God's power to bring the whole project to completion.)

How could these verses encourage you as you work on building a heritage? (If we're partners with God in the process, we can trust the results to Him.)

Philippians 4:4-9, 13

As we work on building a heritage, what should our attitude be? (One of rejoicing rather than worrying. We should come to God with our concerns about the children we love, concentrating on the potential good that can come from our efforts rather than negative possibilities, and He will help us to be at peace.)

If you're feeling overwhelmed by the job of building a heritage, how could verse 13 encourage you? (We can do anything if we rely on God's strength instead of our own.)

❸ Buckle Down

Objective:
To give group members the time and ideas they need to make specific plans to build a heritage for the children they love (20-30 minutes).

Remind your group members that building a heritage for children is a task for both parents and adults that can influence a child's life. Encourage both the parents and "non-parents" in the group to be creative and positive as they build a heritage.

Let group members browse the "smorgasbord" of reproducible sheets you've arranged on a table. Individuals and couples should choose the ones they want to work on in this session and seat themselves in any way that helps them concentrate on the task at hand. Encourage people to begin with "Planning Your Heritage: Getting Started" (RS-11-13A) if possible. The other sheets may be tackled in any order.

As people get to work, wander the room and offer help as needed. Here are suggestions for helping people make the most of the worksheets.

"Planning Your Heritage: Getting Started" (RS-11-13A)

In Part II, where people are to describe the legacies they'd like to leave, urge them to write short summaries rather than trying to list every aspect of their legacies. Concentrating on the question, "When those I love reflect upon the heritage they were given, what do I want them to remember?" should help. If people would like to pause for prayer when they reach Part III, encourage them to do so.

"Family Fragrance Factory" (RS-11-13B)

This exercise will be most effective if participants choose simple actions they can perform every day—simply because such actions will readily become positive habits. Nobody wants to get stuck in a rut, though, so make sure people understand that they aren't committing themselves to do the same things every day for the rest of their lives. A one-month commitment might be reasonable.

"Impression Point Pointers" (RS-11-13C)

A good way to use impression points on a weekly basis is to schedule a weekly Family Night. People may want to follow this worksheet with "Family Night Planner" (RS-11-13H) and turn their impression points into official Family Nights.

If some group members don't have children at home, encourage them to consider how they can use impression points on a weekly or monthly basis with extended family members—even if they live thousands of miles away. For example, a grandparent could send a child a special "care" package once a month. The package might contain a video with a Christian message, a book with accompanying tape on which the grandparent reads the story and makes comments, etc.

"Right Angle Workshop" (RS-11-13D)

If people have trouble narrowing down the principles they'd like to communicate to kids, encourage them to think of issues that have come up recently at home. For example, one child may reject saving up for something valuable in favor of blowing each week's allowance on cheap vending-machine trinkets at the supermarket. In this case, delayed gratification might be a good principle to address. If people are stuck for activity ideas, suggest that they think about seasonal or holiday possibilities that will present themselves during the next six months.

"Writing Your Family Creed" (RS-11-13E)

Provide plenty of paper with this worksheet, and be sure the pencils have erasers! This is among the most challenging exercises. Help people to understand that they aren't writing the Declaration of Independence; their creeds should be in words with which they're comfortable, and need not sound like doctrinal statements. The process should begin with lots of brainstormed ideas that may be discarded later. If you have time to prepare a family creed yourself before the session, you could offer it as a starting point.

"Family Traditions Calendar" (RS-11-13F)

Encourage people to list on the back of the sheet preparations that will be needed for these celebrations—materials, guests to invite, who'll be responsible for doing what, etc. This added step should increase the likelihood that the celebrations will actually take place.

"Marking Your Milestones" (RS-11-13G)

If participants need more ideas for markable milestones, point out that "firsts" aren't the only occasions to celebrate. Making it through a challenge (getting a cast removed from a broken arm, taking the SAT exam, finishing a book report) may deserve celebration. A child's spiritual birthday is also worth marking, even if no one recalls the date on which the original event occurred.

"Family Night Planner" (RS-11-13H)

Let those who use this sheet know that they can get further help with Family Night planning from the book *An Introduction to Family Nights* by Jim Weidmann and Kurt Bruner with Mike and Amy Nappa (Victor Books). This volume, Book 1 in the Family Night Tool Chest series, is packed with more than enough resources for a dozen great Family Nights.

"Leading a Child to Christ, Part I" (RS-11-13I) and "Leading a Child to Christ, Part II" (RS-11-13J)

If possible, have users of these two worksheets work with at least one person outside their own household. Parents who are concerned about their children's salvation need support, and those who have already led a child to Christ may be able to offer encouragement. Rather than writing answers to all the questions on the sheet, participants could tell their answers to those with whom they're working. Be ready to deal with any calls for help that group members make in response to the third question on the "Part II" sheet.

❹ All in This Together

Objective:
To let participants support each other in the heritage-building process by sharing ideas and praying together (15-20 minutes).

After allowing as much time as possible for people to work on the sheets of their choice, regather the whole group. Guide the sharing of results and concerns with questions like the following:

What's one thing you learned today?

Did you encounter any rough spots that the rest of us might be able to help you with?

Did you come up with any heritage-building ideas you can share?

How has it gone during the week as you've been trying some of the things you've learned?

How can we pray for you as you seek to build a heritage?

Allow as much time as you can for group members to pray for each other. Encourage specific prayers for participants who face challenges in heritage building—particularly single parents, those who didn't receive a strong heritage themselves, and those who are trying to overcome a late start in heritage building. Pray for the needs of specific children in the families represented.

If your church can help match adult volunteers with children in single-parent families who need additional role models, be sure to offer this information. If possible, be available after the session to listen to concerns and to steer people toward family counseling resources your church may provide.

At the end of your final session, invite group members to take with them any leftover worksheets that interest them. You may also want to schedule a "reunion" party for the group about six months from now, to see how the heritage-building process is going and to offer added encouragement.

Parental Puzzle

U	R	P	Q	E	W	L	M	S	A	H
Z	Y	T	B	F	E	P	L	N	F	C
W	T	R	H	Y	K	I	L	O	F	B
M	A	C	W	Q	Y	J	K	F	B	U
N	O	L	M	J	H	D	E	G	S	A
F	H	T	R	D	C	L	K	H	U	P
M	N	W	D	X	S	F	G	B	R	G
K	J	Y	A	W	M	X	I	T	J	Y
E	K	N	H	F	V	B	Q	A	F	G
P	I	J	G	K	E	T	G	V	C	X
B	H	W	Z	D	F	L	P	I	Q	S

Find the following words in the grid above and circle them. You may find them horizontally, vertically, or diagonally, backwards or forwards.

PARENT	WISDOM	MOTHER
GUIDANCE	TRAINING	SON
CHILD	HERITAGE	DAUGHTER
SCRIPTURE	FATHER	FUTURE

Instructions to Partner 2 ONLY:

DO NOT tell your partner, but he or she won't find any of the words in the puzzle. It's designed to frustrate him or her. You may not help your partner in any way.

The Reading of the Will

Characters: Ms. Peri Mason, Attorney-at-Law
               Ted Tarbuckle

MASON: Thank you for coming to my office, Mr. Tarbuckle. Are you ready for the reading of your parents' will?

TED: Yes, I guess so.

MASON *(reading)*: Being of sound mind, we hereby bequeath to our son Ted the following items. First, the old toaster in the hall closet that never popped up unless it was hit with a hiking boot…

TED *(wiping away a tear)*: Ah, I remember that toaster.

MASON: Second, our entire collection of souvenir dust bunnies from under the motel beds of all the places we ever went on vacation…

TED: Memories, memories…

MASON: And third, a pair of size 12 hiking boots for hitting the old toaster.

TED *(after a pause)*: And?

MASON: And that's it.

TED: That can't be it! My parents had so much! The house, the car, the diamond mine in Johannesburg…

MASON: Yes, Mr. Tarbuckle. Your parents had many things they could have passed on. But they didn't want to impose their valuables on you.

TED: Impose? How would their valuables be an imposition?

MASON: They weren't sure you'd want their valuables. To tell you the truth, they were a little embarrassed by the valuables they'd inherited. Such old-fashioned valuables, after all. Traditional valuables. Family valuables.

TED: So what happened to it all?

MASON: I don't know. When your parents were gone, so were their valuables.

TED: But those valuables were rightfully mine! I've got to find them! Excuse me! *(He leaves.)*

MASON *(with a sigh)*: They say you can't take it with you…but an awful lot of my clients manage to somehow! *(She exits.)*

Spiritual Legacy Evaluation

Answer each question by circling the number that best reflects the legacy you have received from your parents; then add your total score.

1. To what degree were spiritual principles incorporated into daily family life?
1—Never
2—Rarely
3—Sometimes
4—Frequently
5—Almost always
6—Consistently

2. Which word captures the tone of how you learned to view/relate to God?
1—Absent
2—Adversarial
3—Fearful
4—Casual
5—Solemn
6—Intimate

3. How would you summarize your family's level of participation in spiritual activities?
1—Nonexistent
2—Rare
3—Occasional
4—Regimental
5—Active
6—Enthusiastic

4. How were spiritual discussions applied in your home?
1—They weren't
2—To control
3—To manipulate
4—To teach
5—To influence
6—To reinforce

5. What was the perspective in your home with regard to moral absolutes?
1—If it feels good, do it!
2—There are no absolutes
3—Let your heart guide you
4—Dogmatic legalism
5—Moderate conservatism
6—Clear life boundaries

Results
Above 24 = Strong spiritual legacy
14-18 = Mixed legacy—good and bad elements
Below 10 = Damaged spiritual legacy
19-24 = Healthy legacy
10-13 = Weak spiritual legacy

Emotional Legacy Evaluation

Answer each question by circling the number that best reflects the legacy you have received from your parents; then add your total score.

1. When you walked into your house, what was your feeling?
1—Dread
2—Tension
3—Chaos
4—Stability
5—Calm
6—Warmth

2. Which word best describes the tone of your home?
1—Hateful
2—Angry
3—Sad
4—Serious
5—Relaxed
6—Fun

3. What was the message of your family life?
1—You are worthless.
2—You are a burden.
3—You are OK.
4—You are respected.
5—You are important.
6—You are the greatest.

4. Which word best describes the "fragrance" of your home life?
1—Repulsive
2—Rotten
3—Unpleasant
4—Sterile
5—Fresh
6—Sweet

5. Which was most frequent in your home?
1—An intense fight
2—The silent treatment
3—Detached apathy
4—A strong disagreement
5—A kind word
6—An affectionate hug

Results
Above 24 = Strong emotional legacy
14-18 = Mixed legacy—good and bad elements
Below 10 = Damaged emotional legacy

19-24 = Healthy legacy
10-13 = Weak emotional legacy

Social Legacy Evaluation

Answer each question by circling the number that best reflects the legacy you have received from your parents; then add your total score.

1. Which words most closely resemble the social tone of your family?
1—Cruel and abusive
2—Cutting sarcasm
3—Chaotic and distant
4—Noncommunicative but stable
5—Secure with open communication
6—Loving and fun

2. What was the message of your home life with regard to relationships?
1—"Step on others to get your way."
2—"Hurt them if they hurt you."
3—"Demand your rights."
4—"Mind your own business."
5—"Treat others with respect."
6—"Put others before yourself."

3. How were rules set and enforced in your home?
1—Independent of relationship
2—In reaction to parental stress
3—Dictatorially
4—Inconsistently
5—Out of concern for my well-being
6—In the context of a loving relationship

4. Which word best characterizes the tone of communication in your home?
1—Shouting
2—Manipulation
3—Confusing
4—Clear
5—Constructive
6—Courteous

5. How did your family deal with wrong behavior?
1—Subtle reinforcement
2—Accepted in the name of love
3—Guilt trip
4—Severe punishment
5—Discussion
6—Loving, firm discipline

Results

Above 24 = Strong social legacy
14-18 = Mixed legacy—good and bad elements
Below 10 = Damaged social legacy

19-24 = Healthy legacy
10-13 = Weak social legacy

Used by permission from *The Heritage* by J. Otis Ledbetter and Kurt Bruner,
© 1996 by the authors. Published by ChariotVictor Publishing, a division of Cook Communications.

The Heritage Mixer

How does a couple blend two heritages into one?

Some relationships bring religious differences. "Will we raise the kids Baptist or Presbyterian?" Others bring regional, cultural, or ethnic differences into the marriage. "Will we serve grits or bagels at breakfast?" Whatever the specifics, whether trying to blend minor differences or major disagreements, it is vital that Mom and Dad figure out a way to give a single, united heritage to the kids. And it won't just happen. It must be planned.

There is no magic formula or deeply profound secret to creating a blended heritage. It simply requires a willingness to invest the time and effort needed to make it happen. We recommend the following recipe.

1. Honestly examine your own past heritage. Hopefully, you've already walked through this exercise.

2. Compare your past heritage to your mate's past heritage. List the characteristics side by side to highlight any dramatic differences.

HUSBAND'S HERITAGE	WIFE'S HERITAGE
Spiritual	
Emotional	
Social	

3. List areas of your combined heritage that seem solid.

_____

_____

_____

4. List areas that appear weak and need to be strengthened.

_____

_____

_____

5. Write down the characteristics that you both wish to see included in the heritage given in your home. Come to agreement, even if it requires compromise (and it will). Give and take, so that your children can get something worth taking.

_____

_____

Just One More Thing

Characters: Greg Hassleberry
               Meg Hassleberry

GREG (*quickly and mechanically*): OK, Dear. Let's report on the day. Got your Christian DayFinder?

MEG (*also quickly and mechanically*): Check.

GREG: Had personal quiet time.

MEG: Had devotions as a couple.

GREG: Listened to Christian radio.

MEG: Watched Christian TV.

GREG: At breakfast, drilled kids on memory verses while eating waffles made in shape of crosses.

MEG: Put Christian witness T-shirts on kids and ironed them. In that order.

GREG: On way to work, listened to inspirational Christian tapes; closed eyes while praying for unreached people groups; ran into Honda Civic.

MEG: During the day, performed duties of Proverbs 31 woman: Selected wool and flax, considered field and bought it, grasped spindle with fingers, clothed self in purple…

GREG: After work, spent intense quality time with children, asking how day went and nodding head vigorously while mentally planning next week's Sunday school lesson…

MEG: Over dinner, affirmed worth of each child, discussed Calvinist and non-Calvinist approaches to dispensationalism.

GREG: After dinner: Homework, family devotions from Book of Leviticus, watched Christian video with children followed by bedside prayers for each member of Congress.

MEG: 10 p.m.: Fell into bed, exhausted. (*They slump back in their chairs.*)

GREG: Oh. Just one more thing. They said at church that we have to start building a family heritage.

MEG (*pretending to write in DayFinder*): 3:00 a.m.: Build family heritage.

GREG: And now, from our evening devotional guide, the verse of the day. "Come unto me, all ye that labor and are heavy laden, and I will give you rest." Matthew 11:28.

MEG: You know, I've never understood that verse.

GREG: Neither have I. (*They slump backward and start snoring.*)

Objection, Your Honor!

But I didn't get a good heritage myself. I can't pass one on.

Sure, it may be easier for others. Of course the process will be more difficult for you. But as Booker T. Washington said in his autobiography, *Up from Slavery*, "Success is to be measured not so much by the position one has reached in life, as by the obstacles which he has overcome while trying to succeed."

You can successfully give what you didn't receive. Will it be easy? No. Will it be worth it? You bet!

Talk to anyone who has successfully broken the cycle by giving what he didn't get, and you'll discover that perseverance is the key ingredient. There are very few immediate rewards. Often it takes years to see the fruit of your labor. And since the long-term impact of your efforts is not clear, it is easy to lose heart. But step by step, day by day, one choice at a time, you are making a difference.

But my kids might reject my heritage. Why bother?

One never knows the impact a solid spiritual legacy may have in the lives of our children, or beyond. Your children may reject the legacy, either temporarily or completely. Your duty is only to present them with the truth and leave the results with God.

But I'm not a spiritual giant. I'm not sure I'm the best example.

That's OK. A strong spiritual legacy does not require uncommon piety. The key is the degree to which unseen spiritual realities are recognized and reinforced at home. You can have an impact for good on your children.

But it's just too time-consuming.

Planning, preparing, and then passing along a solid heritage requires time. When a majority of our time is committed to this and that meeting, project, or personal activity, we will be giving leftover time (and little of it) to our children. The remedy? Keep first things first. Be sure to protect the time needed for family in the midst of the daily scurry. Certainly, many important things need to be done. But what could be more important than giving your family the heritage they deserve?

Renee, a mother whose wayward daughter became the victim of a gang shooting, reveals her heartache. "I wish I had taken the time. I wish I would have expended the energy. I wish I could do it again."

Someday you may regret that you didn't make more money, or that you didn't see the world, but you will never regret the bone-weary time you gave to carry, and pass on, that good heritage. Joy awaits at the end, when you hand off the baton to your now-adult children.

But I don't even have kids.

You can give an extended heritage. You can do it if you're an aunt, an uncle, a grandparent, a single adult. The same is true of childless couples, teachers, and the list goes on. Any relative or friend—anyone who knows what a heritage is and wants to extend that heritage into the lives of others—can do so.

Wake-up Call

Characters: THE VOICE
SAMANTHA, age 7
ELI, her father

(VOICE is offstage and unseen throughout; as the skit opens, SAM and ELI sleep on "beds" in their respective rooms.)

VOICE: Sam! Samantha!

SAM *(waking up)*: Huh? What? *(She rubs her eyes and goes to ELI's room.)* Dad—here I am!

ELI *(waking up)*: Samantha? What are you doing out of bed?

SAM: You called me.

ELI: No, I didn't. Now go back to sleep. *(She goes back to bed.)*

VOICE: Samantha!

SAM: What? *(She returns to DAD's room.)* Here I am.

ELI: Samantha, that's enough! Now, you go right back to your bed and let me sleep, or you can forget going to Chuck E. Cheese™ tomorrow! *(She goes back to bed.)*

VOICE: Sam! Samantha!

SAM *(after sighing and returning to Dad's room)*: Here I am.

ELI: All right, young lady—that's it! Why do you keep getting up?

SAM: Because I heard a voice.

ELI: No, you didn't. And there are no monsters under the bed.

SAM: But it was a real voice. I think it was the voice of …God.

ELI: Who?

SAM: God. You know. The Creator of the universe.

ELI *(worried)*: Now, honey, I'm glad you've been paying attention in Sunday school, but you only imagined that God talked to you. He doesn't really talk to people, honey.

SAM: But in the Bible—

ELI: Yes, well…that was then, this is now. So go back to bed. And if you hear any more voices, just ignore them.

SAM: But I…OK. *(She returns to bed.)*

VOICE: Sam…Samantha! *(SAM sits up and looks as if she wants to answer, but finally puts her hands over her ears and lies down.)* Sam! *(pause)* Eli? *(longer pause)* Anybody?

What It Is

What a Spiritual Legacy Is…and Isn't

A spiritual legacy is the process whereby parents model and reinforce the unseen realities of the spiritual life. A spiritual legacy is not church attendance, though involvement in a local body can strengthen the cord. A spiritual legacy is not Bible reading, though scriptural principles are a vital part of spiritual perspective.

A spiritual legacy—like our emotional and social legacies—is influenced far more by the parents' actions and attitudes than by the roles and rules of institutions or by repetitive religious practices.

A solid spiritual legacy is more about the daily grind than it is weekly worship. Our children need to observe the spiritual life as part of normal living rather than the exclusive domain of saintly grandmothers and professional theologians.

A Strong Spiritual Legacy…
• Acknowledges and reinforces spiritual realities.
• Views God as a personal, caring being who is to be both loved and respected
• Makes spiritual activities an integral aspect of life (church attendance, prayer, Scripture reading, etc.).
• Talks about spiritual issues as a means of reinforcing spiritual commitments.
• Clarifies timeless truth, right from wrong.
• Incorporates spiritual principles into everyday living.

A Weak Spiritual Legacy…
• Undermines or ignores spiritual realities.
• Represents God as an impersonal being, to be ignored or feared.
• Never or rarely participates in spiritual activities.
• Has few spiritual discussions of a constructive nature.
• Confuses absolutes and upholds relativism.
• Separates the spiritual from the "practical."

Adapted by permission from *The Heritage* by J. Otis Ledbetter and Kurt Bruner, © 1996 by the authors. Published by ChariotVictor Publishing, a division of Cook Communications.

Home Inspection

FAMILY ROOM
Your kids trust the TV ratings system; you don't, and a battle over what they can watch ensues.

CHILD'S BEDROOM
This one wants a drink of water five times a night.

BATHROOM
Mornings are a traffic jam here.

MASTER BEDROOM
Spouse thinks you're way too easy on the kids and won't speak to you.

ENTRY
The kids keep forgetting to wipe their feet

LIVING ROOM
Whenever guests come, your kids want to hide instead of showing how they can play the theme from "Batman" on the piano like you want them to.

DINING ROOM
Your younger kids kick each other under the table; your teenager wants to argue about getting his nose pierced.

KITCHEN
Your kids demand pizza instead of meatloaf.

CHILD'S BEDROOM
Refuses to pray at bedtime.

TEEN'S BEDROOM
Always messy.

BASEMENT
You want to turn this into a workshop; your spouse wants to make it an office; your kids want it to be a playroom. It's not big enough to be all three.

GARAGE
You promised your teenager he could use the car tonight, but that was before he came home with a "D" in algebra on his report card.

Which of the following principles from I Corinthians 13:4-8 could be applied to settling the conflicts described on the blueprint? Show your answers by writing the applicable principles' numbers in the appropriate rooms.

1. Love is patient
2. Love is kind
3. Love does not envy
4. Love does not boast
5. Love is not proud
6. Love is not rude
7. Love is not self-seeking
8. Love is not easily angered

9. Love keeps no record of wrongs
10. Love does not delight in evil
11. Love rejoices with the truth
12. Love always protects
13. Love always trusts
14. Love always hopes
15. Love always perseveres
16. Love never fails

Just in Case

CASE ONE: THE GIRL WHO WAS DIFFERENT

Since she was a baby, your daughter Nicole has been plagued by ear infections. She's had so many you can't remember them all—along with countless antibiotics and several drainage tubes that had to be inserted in her ears.

Nicole is six years old now, and the infections seem to have tapered off. But on your last visit to the pediatrician, he recommended you take Nicole to an audiologist to have her hearing tested. You did, and the news was bad. Your daughter has a partial—and probably permanent—hearing loss.

The audiologist said Nicole's hearing loss isn't severe enough to require a hearing aid. But she added that Nicole should use an "audio trainer"—a pair of headphones that receives signals from a teacher's lapel microphone—at school.

Now Nicole has to wear headphones whenever she's in class. She tells you she hates them, that all the other kids stare at her because of them. For the last four nights at bedtime she's prayed that she won't have to wear them anymore.

How can you help Nicole deal with this emotional "hit"?

CASE TWO: LASTING IMPACT

Three weeks ago you were driving to the grocery store with your eleven-year-old son Jeremy. Suddenly, at the corner of Lexington and Main, a green pickup ran a stop sign and broadsided your car. You can still feel the horror of glimpsing the truck out of the corner of your eye, the helplessness as it kept coming, the sickening invasion of what you thought was your safe zone.

You can still feel the fear, too—the fear you felt as you realized the truck had hit Jeremy's side of the car. Bits of glass clinked to the pavement as you turned to see whether he was alive. Thankfully, he was—though he was staring straight ahead, a cut on his lip starting to bleed. Both of you were numb until the police came; Jeremy started shivering then, but later seemed to be all right. Your car, on the other hand, was totaled.

It soon became apparent that Jeremy was not okay. He has nightmares about the accident almost every night, and gets a stomach ache when he has to ride in the car you've borrowed. The other day he started shaking again when you drove through the intersection where the accident happened. He's afraid to ride the bus to school.

How can you help Jeremy deal with this emotional "hit"?

Repairing the Stabilizer Bar

1. *Recognize and divert the impact of the pain.* This means creating an environment of extra understanding and safety for the child so that healing can begin.

2. *Repair the damage.* Only God can do this completely, but we can help by telling the truth. For instance, the truth is that the incident happened; healing will come; the child is accepted; God cares, and hates what happened.

3. *Give the child a place of rest, not rescue.* Much as we might like to, we can't and shouldn't protect children from every pain. There are some things children must struggle through to mature. Our responsibility is to give them a safe place to learn and a loving environment in which emotional maturity can grow.

Adapted by permission from *The Heritage* by J. Otis Ledbetter and Kurt Bruner, © 1996 by the authors. Published by ChariotVictor Publishing, a division of Cook Communications.

Fault Lines

Characters: NARRATOR, MOM, PROSECUTOR, JUDGE

NARRATOR *(in a Rod Serling-like voice)*: You're entering another dimension—a dimension of guilt, of regret, of really weird theme music. Watch out for that signpost up ahead; you're entering The Every Parent's Worst Nightmare Zone.

PROSECUTOR: Tell me, Mrs. McCleaver…do you recognize the defendant?

MOM *(sadly)*: Of course. He's my son.

PROSECUTOR: Are you aware that your son has been charged with petty larceny, grand theft auto, mail fraud, assault with a deadly weapon, espionage, and driving under the influence of a cellular phone?

MOM *(tearfully)*: Yes.

PROSECUTOR: Mrs. McCleaver, where were you on the night of August 16, 1987?

MOM: I—I'm not sure…

PROSECUTOR *(accusing)*: Isn't it true that you were blow-drying your hair? And isn't it true that your blow dryer caused the electrical system of your home to blow a fuse?

MOM: Well, maybe I—

PROSECUTOR *(louder)*: And isn't it true that when the power went out, your son was unable to play Nintendo as he had planned?

MOM: I-I—

PROSECUTOR *(still louder)*: And isn't it true that being unable to play Nintendo caused your son to be…disappointed?

MOM: I suppose he—

PROSECUTOR *(practically shouting)*: And isn't it true, Mrs. McCleaver, that being disappointed on that horrible night turned your son into the homicidal maniac he is today?

MOM *(sobbing)*: Yes! Yes! I did it! It's my fault—all my fault!

PROSECUTOR: No further questions, your honor. *(Exits.)*

JUDGE: Mrs. McCleaver, you are hereby declared guilty.

MOM: Of what?

JUDGE: Everything! The defendant is free to go.

MOM *(tearfully)*: If only I'd known! I never would have dried my hair—never! *(She collapses, sobbing.)*

NARRATOR: Mrs. June McCleaver—a woman with very wet eyes…and very dry hair. Submitted for your self-recrimination…from The Every Parent's Worst Nightmare Zone.

Box Socials

Building Blocks
1. Respect
2. Responsibility
3. Love and Acceptance
4. Borders

Rules within Relationship

As you set borders, keep one caution in mind. Because they are typically expressed as rules, borders are respected best when they are given with love. Jason, for example, learned right from wrong while growing up. But the moment he became old enough to make his own decisions, he rejected most of the values Mom and Dad had taught. What went wrong?

The primary reason was that rules were given in a relational vacuum. Jason's parents gave the right medicine, but it wasn't served with the spoonful of sugar, namely, strong relationship. For whatever reasons, they were distant. They loved Jason but had a hard time demonstrating it. Honest, open communication was difficult, so it rarely occurred. Jason was not given a forum in which to discuss, ask, question, or challenge Mom and Dad's "list." The inevitable result? Rebellion.

Leading Social Legacy Indicators

A Strong Social Legacy…
- Sets clear "borders" on how to appropriately treat others.
- Teaches respect for all people.
- Instills a sense of responsibility for the feelings and property of others.
- Balances unconditional love for the person with conditional acceptance of behavior.
- Enforces rules in the context of a loving relationship.
- Models clear and sensitive communication skills.

A Weak Social Legacy…
- Causes confusion regarding what is appropriate treatment and what is not.
- Treats others with disrespect.
- Follows a "survival of the fittest" perspective.
- Accepts wrong behavior in the name of love.
- Is dictatorial, enforcing rules for their own sake.
- Models poor interpersonal communication.

Making Scents

SCENE 1: AFFECTION

Parent: You used to like walking your second grader to school. You even got to give him a kiss at the door. But lately he turns away when you try that. If you ask for a high-five instead, he punches your hand as if to show the other kids how tough he is. You want to say goodbye affectionately, but aren't sure how.

Child: Getting a kiss in front of the other kids is embarrassing. You're not a baby anymore. Why can't your parent let you walk to school alone? Your friend Jeff gets to!

SCENE 2: RESPECT

Parent: You've just heard that one of your teenager's friends has been arrested for selling marijuana. You haven't noticed any signs of drug use by your teenager, but you're no expert. She does spend a lot of time in her room. And there was that slip from a B to a C in English last semester. You're standing in the middle of her room, thinking about searching for drugs, when your teenager comes in and asks what you're doing.

Child: You're bummed out about your friend's arrest. But you haven't used any drugs. You think your parents are paranoid. And don't they understand they shouldn't be coming into your room without permission?

SCENE 3: ORDER

Parent: You're trying to get your fourth grader out the door before the school bus arrives. But that's not easy, since your child got up half an hour late after being awakened by a bad dream last night. Your child forgot to do his homework, too, and is trying to finish it on the kitchen table when he accidentally spills milk all over it. The bus will be here in five minutes; your child is only half dressed, and you can't find any cash for his lunch. If you have to drive him to school, you'll be late for work. And since this has happened three times in the last two weeks, your boss won't like it.

Child: You don't think it's your fault that you're late. You couldn't help it that a bad dream kept you awake. And why can't your parent drive you to school every day? Wouldn't that make things a lot easier?

SCENE 4: MERRIMENT

Parent: You had an awful day at work. All you want to do is eat comfort food and crawl under a blanket. But as soon as you come through the door, your spouse reminds you that you need to prepare dinner and take care of your child all evening because your spouse has a committee meeting at church. The moment your spouse leaves, your preschooler starts pelting you with knock-knock jokes. You're not in the mood.

Child: You heard a bunch of great knock-knock jokes at preschool today. You could hardly wait to get home and tell them. Why doesn't anybody want to hear them? Why is everybody so serious?

SCENE 5: AFFIRMATION

Parent: Your sixth grader just came home from school with a frown and a certificate. The Science Fair awards were presented today, and the "Interesting Invertebrates" project your child worked so hard to finish garnered only an honorable mention. You want to affirm your child's effort, but you're also concerned that she is a perfectionist who can't seem to settle for less than first place. She has threatened to tear up the certificate, stomped off to her room, and shut the door.

Child: You think only stupid kids get honorable mentions. Your project deserved at least second place. The top winners probably got help from their parents. You're sure you'll spend the rest of your life as a loser.

Aromatic Actions

1. AFFECTION
As a result of our discussion, this week I will improve the expression of affection in our home by…
a. Dotting the I's in all my handwriting with little heart shapes.
b. Urging everyone to watch reruns of "The Love Boat."
c. Sneaking up on family members and hugging them until they scream and run away.
d. Yelling at anyone who fails to be sufficiently affectionate to me.
e. Other:

2. RESPECT
As a result of our discussion, this week I will encourage family members to respect each other by…
a. Saying, "Hey, respect each other" a lot.
b. Playing a recording of Aretha Franklin's song "Respect" in the background 24 hours a day.
c. Humiliating them in public if they refuse to recognize each person's worth as a human being.
d. Arming each of them with first-strike nuclear capability.
e. Other:

3. ORDER
As a result of our discussion, this week I will increase the amount of order in our home by…
a. Alphabetizing the jars in the spice rack.
b. Requiring each person to sort his or her garbage according to color, density, and specific gravity.
c. Hiring off-duty police officers to patrol the hallway after "lights out."
d. Installing metal detectors.
e. Other:

4. MERRIMENT
As a result of our discussion, this week I will help to create an atmosphere of merriment in our home by…
a. Wearing a bright but tasteful smiley-face button on my lapel.
b. Hiring a clown.
c. Making milk come out of my nose at the dinner table.
d. Ordering everyone to laugh at six-minute intervals.
e. Other:

5. AFFIRMATION
As a result of our discussion, this week I will affirm each family member by…
a. Trying to remember his or her name.
b. Saying, "You're not as ugly as you were yesterday."
c. Laying hands on his or her head and making the sound of a trumpet fanfare.
d. Giving him or her a million dollars.
e. Other:

Days of Our Lives

What does your family usually do on Wednesday at 7 p.m.? Go to church? Watch a certain TV show? Shampoo the parrot? For each day of the week, think of one thing your family (or part of your family) tends to do at a particular time. Draw a symbol to represent each activity. Then, next to each symbol, write a T if you think of that activity as a tradition. Write an H if it's just a habit. If it's an activity you'd like to get rid of, draw an X over the symbol. If it's an activity that might be used to teach a spiritual truth, circle the symbol.

6							
7							
8							
9							
10							
11							
12							
1							
2							
3							
4							
5							
6							
7							
8							
9							
10							

Take It on Home

Every family has traditions—some by design, others by default. Those who seek to give a strong heritage understand the powerful impact of traditions on the identity of their children. Take a few moments to evaluate the use of tradition in your home.

1. How well have you developed meaningful tradition in your home? Rate yourself in the following categories. Grade your home from one to five for each, five being highest.

Events—
How enjoyable and meaningful have you made periodic events (holidays, game nights, etc.) in your home?
1   2   3   4   5

Stories—
How often do you tell the stories of your home, giving your loved ones a strong connection to past and present family history?
1   2   3   4   5

Creed—
Does your family have a clear, well-defined belief system that is refined, recorded, and referenced?
1   2   3   4   5

2. If you haven't already done so, prepare a first draft of your family creed—those foundational beliefs upon which your home is established. Once completed, evaluate how well your family traditions have reinforced those beliefs.

3. Identify one area for each category of tradition which you can implement over the coming months which will serve to establish and reinforce a strong sense of identity with your kids.

Events—
I will plan and prepare for the following event…

I will use this event as an opportunity to reinforce…

Stories—
I will tell the following story from the life of our family…

Creed—
I will refine, record, or reference our family creed by…

Plumb Lines

In each of the following "right angle" areas, look up the passage to find a standard upheld by God's Word. Then draw lines to indicate how far off you think our society's standards are from the biblical norm (that norm being represented by the vertical "plumb" line).

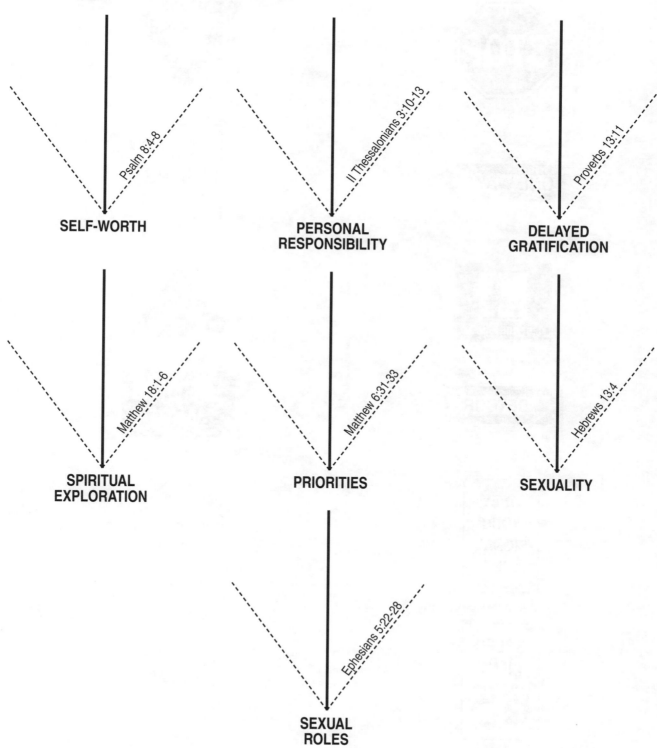

SELF-WORTH

Psalm 8:4-8

PERSONAL RESPONSIBILITY

II Thessalonians 3:10-13

DELAYED GRATIFICATION

Proverbs 13:11

SPIRITUAL EXPLORATION

Matthew 18:1-6

PRIORITIES

Matthew 6:31-33

SEXUALITY

Hebrews 13:4

SEXUAL ROLES

Ephesians 5:22-28

Sign Here

Which of these signs *best* communicates a "right angle" message you want to give to a child (or children) you love this week? Write their names next to the sign, and notes on what message you'd like to give with it.

Remodel your home to illustrate what life was like in Bible times.

Combine picnicking and fasting.

Let siblings practice baptism while they wash the dishes.

Demonstrate Ezekiel's wheel-within-a-wheel in the living room.

Feign terminal illness so you can deliver a daily sermonette from your "deathbed."

Tell scary evangelistic stories to preschoolers at bedtime.

R.S.V.P.

1. Your older sister Amy, a Christian, died two weeks ago. Today your six-year-old daughter asks you, "What do you think Aunt Amy is doing in heaven right now?"

🗨 VERBAL RESPONSE

★ SYMBOLIC RESPONSE

👁 VISUAL RESPONSE

✏ WRITTEN RESPONSE

2. Your nine-year-old son is in a club program at church that emphasizes memorizing Bible verses. Right now the club is offering a prize to every child who memorizes the order of the books of the Bible. Your son wants the prize, but can't seem to get beyond the first six books or so.

🗨 VERBAL RESPONSE

★ SYMBOLIC RESPONSE

👁 VISUAL RESPONSE

✏ WRITTEN RESPONSE

3. Your 15-year-old son likes to surf the World Wide Web. You installed a program on your computer to keep him from accessing Internet pornography, but yesterday you discovered a printout in the garbage that indicates he's found a way around the site-blocking software.

🗨 VERBAL RESPONSE

★ SYMBOLIC RESPONSE

👁 VISUAL RESPONSE

✏ WRITTEN RESPONSE

4. Your four-year-old daughter recently prayed to receive Jesus as her Savior. You're happy about that, but wonder how much she really understands. Today she asked you, "Is Jesus little? He must be, if He lives in my heart."

🗨 VERBAL RESPONSE

★ SYMBOLIC RESPONSE

👁 VISUAL RESPONSE

✏ WRITTEN RESPONSE

Planning Your Heritage: Getting Started

RS- 11-13A

I. Who Will Receive From You?

Identify the people in your life to whom you wish to give a heritage. If you are married with children, the priority is obvious. But the extended heritage is also a vital part of what you give, especially if you are single, childless, or beyond the child-rearing years. For example, you may identify Sally, that little girl in your Sunday school class at church. Or perhaps Chuck, the child of a single mom, who needs a strong male role model in his life.

To whom do you seek to give a strong heritage? List their names below.

Family members: _____

Others: _____

II. What You Want to Give

Now set your goal. As you draft your goal, ask yourself this question: "When those I love reflect upon the heritage they were given, what do I want them to remember?" Use the back of this sheet if needed.

The Spiritual Legacy I/we want to give: _____
_____
_____

The Emotional Legacy I/we want to give: _____
_____
_____

The Social Legacy I/we want to give: _____
_____
_____

III. Seeking Help

Before you go any farther, take some time to talk with God. Admit your weaknesses with regard to the heritage process. Confess where you've failed, and ask for help as you seek to make a fresh start. Ask Him to give you the wisdom and strength needed to break the cycle and give what you didn't get. You may even need to ask Him to help you overcome a selfish or apathetic attitude. He will come alongside as you begin the heritage-building process, if you ask Him. Use the space below to write a prayer of commitment and petition for wisdom before you begin building your detailed plan.

Dear Lord: _____
_____
_____
_____

A second source of help is other people. There are others around you who have passed along, or are now passing, a solid heritage. Spend time with them. Learn from them. Ask questions. Steal ideas! Think of two to four individuals who may be a source of help along the way and plan to meet with them.

My two to four "Heritage Consultants":
_____
_____

Family Fragrance Factory

The goal of the family fragrance is to create an ongoing environment of love in the home. We recommend that you identify *daily* activities and patterns in the home which create a sweet-smelling aroma.

Think of a "fragrant" daily habit you can form in each of the following areas. Write it down. Post your list in a spot where you'll see it every morning until your new habits are part of your daily routine.

Every day I will demonstrate affection by _____

_____.

Examples: Kissing my spouse in front of the kids; giving the kids a high-five before they leave the house; putting a note in my son's lunchbox or sock drawer; hugging my daughter after she brushes her teeth at night; saying "I love you" at lights-out time.

Every day I will assure respect for the individual by _____

_____.

Examples: Not allowing rude nicknames; getting permission before entering my daughter's room; making time to hear how my spouse's day went; letting my son pick out his own clothes, even if the color combinations aren't perfect; not watching TV sitcoms that glorify insults.

Every day I will create a sense of order by _____

_____.

Examples: Keeping up with the dirty dishes; making sure we've all sat down at the table and prayed before we start eating; not questioning my spouse's disciplinary decisions in front of the kids; making sure homework is done before the TV goes on; listening patiently to a child's request before deciding whether to say yes or no.

Every day I will foster merriment by _____

_____.

Examples: Reading the newspaper comics together; letting the kids call me humorous (but not rude) nick-names; asking whether anybody had a funny dream during the night; playing peek-a-boo with the baby; encouraging the kids to share jokes they heard during the day.

Every day I will give affirmation by _____

_____.

Examples: Thanking the kids whenever they complete a chore; looking at their school papers and posting the best ones on the refrigerator; complimenting them on getting along instead of waiting for a fight to break out; saying something nice about my spouse at the dinner table; encourage my child's ability to make something great of the day when waking him or her in the morning.

Impression Point Pointers

Impression points are used to impress your values upon others. Incidental impression points will occur at any time, but we recommend intentionally creating at least one impression point on a *weekly* basis.

Here are some examples to get you started.

Verbal: Telling your child a story about what happened to you once when you told a lie; making up a song that helps your child memorize a Bible passage.

Symbolic: Challenging your child to put toothpaste back into the tube, thereby illustrating how hard it is to take back hurtful things we've said; taking your child's punishment yourself, as an example of what Jesus did for us.

Visual: Hanging two very different pictures of Jesus on the wall and asking which your child likes better and why; mopping the floor when you'd rather watch TV, as an example of setting priorities.

Written: Writing a letter to your child on his or her birthday, praising his or her accomplishments and spiritual growth in the last year; drawing up a "contract" with your child, in which he or she pledges to do something (listen at church, tell you if he or she has problems at school, avoid premarital sex, etc.) and you agree to provide support or reward.

Now give it a try yourself.

Here are five points I'd like to make during the next four weeks:

1.
2.
3.
4.

To communicate these messages, I will create impression points through the following...

Week One

Why (your point): _____

What (name activity): _____

When (day and time of the week): _____

How (description and preparation): _____
_____

Week Two

Why (your point): _____

What (name activity): _____

When (day and time of the week): _____

How (description and preparation): _____
_____

Week Three

Why (your point): _____

What (name activity): _____

When (day and time of the week): _____

How (description and preparation): _____
_____

Week Four

Why (your point): _____

What (name activity): _____

When (day and time of the week): _____

How (description and preparation): _____
_____

Adapted by permission from *The Heritage* by J. Otis Ledbetter and Kurt Bruner, © 1996 by the authors. Published by ChariotVictor Publishing, a division of Cook Communications.

Right Angle Workshop

Holding up a "right angle" standard means instilling a sense of what is normal and healthy in areas such as self-worth, personal responsibility, delayed gratification, spiritual exploration, priorities, sexuality, and sexual roles. We need to model these principles consistently, but it's helpful to develop a plan for emphasizing each on a *monthly* basis. Once you've identified your list of right-angle principles, plan to focus on one every month throughout the year.

Here are some examples to get your creative juices flowing.

Principle: If you start a job, stick with it until it's complete.
Possible plans: Care for neighbors' dog while they're on vacation; bring child to the office and pay him or her to seal envelopes for large mailing; create special area in garden for child to plant and raise pumpkins.

Principle: God wants us to share with those who don't have enough.
Possible plans: As a family, distribute homemade cookies at nearby nursing home; take field trip to rescue mission; each child donates a toy to church nursery; hold garage sale and give proceeds to hunger relief.

Now choose right-angle principles and plans for the next six months and write them in the following spaces.

Month _____ Principle: _____

Plan: _____

Month _____ Principle: _____

Plan: _____

Month _____ Principle: _____

Plan: _____

Month _____ Principle: _____

Plan: _____

Month _____ Principle: _____

Plan: _____

Month _____ Principle: _____

Plan: _____

Writing Your Family Creed

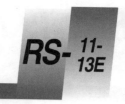

If you haven't already done so, prepare a first draft of your family creed—those foundational beliefs upon which your home is established. Here are helps for getting started. Use separate paper for your responses.

I. What Our Family Believes about God

Here's one version of the historic Apostles' Creed. Try writing your own version, putting it in your own words and adding things you want your children to know about God. For example, how do you hope they see His personality and His desire to relate to them?

"I believe in God, the Father almighty, creator of heaven and earth; I believe in Jesus Christ His only Son our Lord; He was conceived by the power of the Holy Spirit, and born of the Virgin Mary, He suffered under Pontius Pilate, was crucified, died, and was buried. He descended to the dead. On the third day He rose again. He ascended into heaven, and is seated at the right hand of the Father. He will come again to judge the living and the dead. I believe in the Holy Spirit, the holy universal Church, the communion of saints, the forgiveness of sins, the resurrection of the body, and the life everlasting. Amen."

II. What Our Family Believes about the Bible and the Church

What role do you think the Bible should have in the lives of family members?

How do you want family members to be involved in church, and what do you hope they gain from that involvement?

III. What Our Family Believes about Relationships

In ten words or less, how do you want family members to treat each other?

In ten words or less, what do you think is a family member's responsibility to your community? Your country? The world?

IV. What Our Family Believes about Our Mission

In ten words or less, what do you think is the mission of family members as individuals?

In ten words or less, what do you think should be the mission of your family as a whole?

V. What Our Family Believes about Character and Morality

List five qualities all members of your family need to exhibit more and more as they grow.

List five behaviors you think all family members should avoid.

VI. What Our Family Believes about Other Issues

What other issues would you like your family creed to mention? Try writing a one-sentence position statement on each issue. Here are some topics you may want to address: How family decisions are to be made; how conflicts are to be resolved; the kind of atmosphere you want in your home; obedience to parental, school, and other authorities; parents' responsibilities to children.

After completing these six sections, try combining them into a one-page document. If your children are old enough, have them read the result and make suggestions. When your creed is done, post it prominently at home. Make it part of your own life; refer to it when making family decisions and when kids need to know the "why" behind a rule. And be open to changing it as your family grows.

Family Traditions Calendar

Family traditions reinforce a child's sense of personal and family identity. Here's a chance to plan how you'll celebrate some events during the coming year, making them a meaningful part of your family traditions. Circle one example for each month and brainstorm how you'll celebrate it—either using an existing family tradition or creating a new one.

January
New Year's Day, Super Bowl Party
How we'll celebrate:

February
Groundhog Day, Valentine's Day, "I Can't Stand Another Day of Winter" Day, President's Day
How we'll celebrate:

March
St. Patrick's Day, First Day of Spring, Clean the Garage Day
How we'll celebrate:

April
Passion Week, Passover, Good Friday, Easter
How we'll celebrate:

May
Mother's Day, Memorial Day, Mow the Grass Day
How we'll celebrate:

June
Father's Day, First Day of Summer, Flag Day, School's Out Day
How we'll celebrate:

July
Independence Day, Backyard Tent Sleepover, Camping Trip
How we'll celebrate:

August
"Random Acts of Love" Day, Family Baseball Series, End of Summer Party
How we'll celebrate:

September
Labor Day, Back to School Day, First Day of Fall, Rosh Hashana, New Friend Day
How we'll celebrate:

October
Yom Kippur, Reformation Day, Halloween
How we'll celebrate:

November
Thanksgiving, Family Game Showdown, Veterans Day, Election Day
How we'll celebrate:

December
Hannukah, Christmas, Post Holiday "Beat the Blues" Day, New Year's Eve
How we'll celebrate:

Adapted by permission from *The Heritage* by J. Otis Ledbetter and Kurt Bruner, © 1996 by the authors. Published by ChariotVictor Publishing, a division of Cook Communications.

Marking Your Milestones

RS- 11-13G

Not every special day is noted on the calendar. The best tool for affirmation is celebration, so celebrate everything. The specifics are not nearly as important as the objective—to celebrate big and small events in the lives of your children.

Here are just a few ideas. You could celebrate a child's first…

Word	Night away from home	Immunization	Show and tell
Sentence	Report card	Part in a play	Speech
Doctor visit	Paycheck	Finger painting	Bike ride
Dentist visit	Choir concert	Verse memorized	Shave
Driving lesson	Horseback ride	Prayer	Whistle
Soccer game	Step	Apology	Room cleaning
Spelling test	Drink from a cup	Job interview	Meal cooked
Date	Taste of broccoli	Shower	Letter written
Music lesson	Book read aloud	Haircut	Algebra exam

What milestones are coming up during the next year for your children (or children to whom you'd like to pass your heritage)? How will you celebrate?

Child	Milestones Expected During the Coming Year	Celebration Plan

Family Night Planner

Jim's kids are all standing at the foot of the stairs. Dad is at the top of that same staircase. They wait eagerly for instructions. Tonight is "Family Night" at the Weidmann home—a weekly ritual in which Dad spends time intentionally impressing his values on the family. "Here is the assignment. I'll take everyone to Baskin Robbins who is able to get to where I am from down there." He has the attention of all four kids. "But there are a few rules. First, you can't touch the stairs. Second, you can't touch the railing. Now, begin!"

After several contemplative moments, the youngest speaks up. "That's impossible, Dad! How can we get to where you are without touching the stairs or the railing?" After some disgruntled agreement from two of the other children, the oldest gets an idea. "Hey, Dad. Come down here." Jim walks down the stairs. "Now bend over while I get on your back. OK, climb the stairs."

Of course, the plan works. Jim proceeds to parallel the solution to this game with how it is impossible to get to God on our own. "When we let God do the work on our behalf, we can get to heaven," Jim explains. After a trip up the stairs on Dad's back, the whole gang piles into the minivan for a double scoop of mint chocolate chip.

Family Night is a method being used in more and more homes and is one of the best concepts we've encountered for successfully impressing values on kids.

Adapted by permission from *The Heritage* by J. Otis Ledbetter and Kurt Bruner, © 1996 by the authors. Published by ChariotVictor Publishing, a division of Cook Communications.

It's time to plan a Family Night for your family. Check off your choices on the following "menu" (or come up with totally new ideas) to create an evening that would fit your clan. Then, on the back of this sheet, list the preparations you'll need to make and who'll be responsible for each step. Pick a night—and follow through!

Theme: The importance of reading the Bible

Warm-up (choose one):
_____ Hide all the Bibles in the house and see who can find them. Then ask why the Bible is worth looking for.
_____ Run a relay race. Then point out that many people have run a "relay" over the centuries to pass God's Word on to us.

Prayer (choose one):
_____ Have a parent pray, asking God to help you all learn and have fun together.
_____ Have a child pray for a relative or friend who is sick or needs help.

Activity (choose one):
_____ Cook something complicated together without looking at the cookbook. Leave out a key ingredient. When it doesn't turn out quite right, explain that we need to keep reading our "cookbook" (the Bible) for guidance, even if we've read it before.
_____ Instead of cooking something, try making a plastic model (car, spacecraft, etc.) without looking at the instructions.
_____ Take a walk in the dark together with flashlights, but for the first couple of minutes don't let anybody use the lights. When kids get frustrated or anxious, use the lights and explain that the Bible is "a lamp to my feet and a light for my path" (Ps. 119:105), but only if we use it.

Bible Discussion (choose one):
_____ Psalm 119:97-102
_____ II Timothy 3:16-17
_____ For young children, read an action-oriented episode from a Bible story book; talk about how the Bible is full of true stories about amazing people and events.

Refreshments (choose as many as you have room for):
_____ Something with honey in it (see Psalm 119:103)
_____ Sheet cake decorated to look like a Bible
_____ Something "light" (see Psalm 119:105)

Leading a Child to Christ, Part I

The physical and emotional needs of a child are readily apparent, evidenced through their outward behavior. Parents can respond to these needs in tangible ways, touching the child through the five senses, which serve as our gateway to the human soul.

When it comes to making the spiritual connection, however, only God has a direct gateway into the human heart. He has created us with the capacity and desire to relate to Him. He doesn't need the five senses to speak to us. He is able to bypass our senses and go directly to the spirit. But he is the only One who can.

The job of a parent is to understand this dynamic, recognize it when it occurs, and reinforce the unseen connection of the spiritual life. We can encourage our children to pray, listen to their questions about God, and recognize that they may be ready to hear about and understand spiritual matters sooner than we think.

—*J. Otis Ledbetter and Kurt Bruner*

Is the Child Ready?

1. Have you talked with the child about praying to receive Jesus as Savior? If so, what happened?

2. Try to imagine how the child might answer the following questions, based on what you've observed.

• Who is God?
• Who is Jesus?
• How do you think God feels about you?
• Have you ever done anything wrong?
• How do you think God feels about that?
• How do you feel about that?
• Is there anything we can do about that?

3. Based on your answers to the above, how would you rate the child's readiness to put his or her trust in Christ?

_____ He or she doesn't seem capable of understanding these concepts yet.
_____ He or she could understand, but needs more information.
_____ He or she knows the basics, but hasn't taken this step on his or her own as far as I know.
_____ He or she knows the basics but resists taking this step.

4. Based on your answer to (3), which of the following does the child seem to need at this point?

_____ Time to develop the ability to understand.
_____ More information about God, Jesus, right and wrong, and how to start a relationship with God.
_____ Gentle encouragement to act on what he or she knows.
_____ Prayer that God will communicate with him or her in ways that I haven't been able to.

5. Based on your answer to (4), what do you think you need to do next? How will you do it?

Leading a Child to Christ, Part II

Are You Ready?

1. If your child (or another child, if you want to extend your heritage) asks questions that could lead to a discussion of how to receive Jesus as Savior, what will you say? To help you prepare, read the following Bible passages. Then paraphrase each passage *in words that you think the child could understand and that you would be comfortable saying.*

Romans 3:23
Your paraphrase:

I John 1:9
Your paraphrase:

John 3:16
Your paraphrase:

Acts 16:31
Your paraphrase:

2. Which of the following words best describes your feelings about leading your child (or another) to Christ? Choose all that apply.

Scared	**Worried**	**Uninterested**	**Unprepared**
Excited	**Impatient**	**Defeated**	**Nervous**
Unsupported	**Confused**	**Happy**	**Calm**

3. How could the group help you further in this area? Please share your answer with the group leader(s) in person or as a note written in the space below.

Other Products
in the Heritage Builders Series

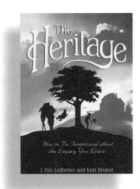

THE HERITAGE
J.Otis Ledbetter & Kurt Bruner
ISBN: 1-56476-694-2
PAPERBACK
RETAIL: $10.99 (U.S.)

THE FAMILY FRAGRANCE
J.Otis & Gail Hover Ledbetter
ISBN: 1-56476-696-9
PAPERBACK
RETAIL: $9.99 (U.S.)

AVAILABLE OCTOBER 1998

FAMILY TRADITIONS
J.Otis Ledbetter & Tim Smith
ISBN: 1-56476-753-1
PAPERBACK
RETAIL: $9.99 (U.S.)

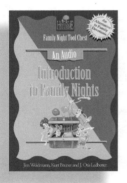

FAMILY NIGHTS AUDIO
ISBN: 6-12501-258-1
AUDIO BLISTER PACK
RETAIL: $5.99 (U.S.)

HERITAGE BUILDERS VIDEO
ISBN: 6-12501-259-X
VIDEO SLEEVE
RETAIL: $9.99 (U.S.)

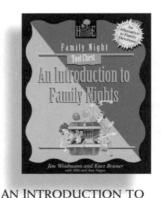

AN INTRODUCTION TO FAMILY NIGHTS
Jim Weidmann & Kurt Bruner
ISBN: 0-78140-096-1
PAPERBACK
RETAIL: $13.99 (U.S.)

BASIC CHRISTIAN BELIEF
Jim Weidmann & Kurt Bruner
ISBN: 0-78140-097-X
PAPERBACK
RETAIL: $13.99 (U.S.)

CHRISTIAN CHARACTER QUALITIES
Jim Weidmann & Kurt Bruner
ISBN: 0-78143-014-3
PAPERBACK
RETAIL: $13.99 (U.S.)

WISDOM LIFE SKILLS
Jim Weidmann & Kurt Bruner
ISBN: 0-78143-015-1
PAPERBACK
RETAIL: $13.99 (U.S.)

MONEY MATTERS FAMILY NIGHTS
Jim Weidmann & Kurt Bruner with Money Matters for Kids™
ISBN: 1-56476-736-1
PAPERBACK
RETAIL: $13.99 (U.S.)

AVAILABLE SEPTEMBER 1998

HOLIDAY FAMILY NIGHT
Jim Weidman, Kurt Bruner & R Wilson
ISBN: 1-56476-737-X
PAPERBACK
RETAIL: $13.99 (U.S.)